WESTWOOD SCHOOL LIBRARY
Santa Clara Unified School District
Santa Clara, California

D0826019

3 3358 00536 0030

Snapshots
Literacy Minilessons Up Close

LINDA HOYT

HEINEMANN
Portsmouth, NH

Heinemann
A division of Reed Elsevier Inc.
361 Hanover Street
Portsmouth, NH 03801-3912
www.heinemann.com

Offices and agents throughout the world

Copyright © 2000 by Linda Hoyt. All rights reserved. No part of this book may be reproduced in any form or by any electronic or mechanical means, including information storage and retrieval systems, without permission in writing from the publisher, except by a reviewer, who may quote brief passages in a review. Copyrighted forms throughout the book may be photocopied for classroom use only.

Excerpts from *The Burning Questions of Bingo Brown* by Betsy Byars. Copyright © 1988 by Betsy Byars. Used by permission of Viking Penguin, a division of Penguin Putnam, Inc.

Excerpt from *Mrs. Wishy Washy Brown* by Joy Crowley. Copyright © by The Wright Group, 19201 120th Avenue NE, Botnell, Washington 98011. Used by permission of The Wright Group.

Excerpt from "Jelly Fact" by Paul Duchene of The Oregonian. Sunday, December 26, 1999. Copyright © 1999 by The Oregonian, Oregonian Publishing Company. All rights reserved. Reprinted with permission.

"Born of a Tough Country" by Tom Hallman of The Oregonian. Monday, December 27, 1999. Copyright © 1999 by The Oregonian, Oregonian Publishing Company. All rights reserved. Reprinted with permission.

"Nasty Weather Delays Plans to Let Keiko Stretch. Flukes, Violent Winds, and Massive Tidal Surges Hamper the Setup of a Custom-Made Barrier Net for the Orca in an Iceland Bay" by Katy Muldoon of The Oregonian. Tuesday, December 28, 1999. Copyright © 1999 by The Oregonian, Oregonian Publishing Company. All rights reserved. Reprinted with permission.

Excerpts and illustrations from *Amazing Sharks* by Melvin Berger. Copyright © 1995 by Newbridge Communications. Used by permission of Newbridge Educational Publishing, New York, NY.

Excerpts and illustrations from *Fly Butterfly* by Brenda Parkes. Copyright © 1999 by Newbridge Communications. Used by permission of Newbridge Educational Publishing, New York, NY.

Excerpts and illustrations from *What Can Fly* by Brenda Parkes. Copyright © 1999 by Newbridge Communications. Used by permission of Newbridge Educational Publishing, New York, NY.

Excerpts and illustrations from *Taking Care of Baby* by Christine Economos. Copyright © 1999 by Newbridge Communications. Used by permission of Newbridge Educational Publishing, New York, NY.

Excerpts and illustrations from *The Coral Reef* by Christine Economos. Copyright © 1999 by Newbridge Communications. Used by permission of Newbridge Educational Publishing, New York, NY.

Excerpts from *Hatchet* by Gary Paulsen are reprinted with the permission of Simon & Schuster Books for Young Readers, an imprint of Simon & Schuster Children's Publishing Division. Copyright © 1987 by Gary Paulsen.

Library of Congress Cataloging-in-Publication Data

Hoyt, Linda.
    Snapshots : literacy minilessons up close / Linda Hoyt ; [edited by Lois Bridges].
        p. cm.
    Includes bibliographical references.
    ISBN 0-325-00272-X (alk. paper)
    1. Reading (Primary) 2. Literacy. I. Title: Literacy minilessons up close. II. Bird, Lois Bridges. III. Title.

    LB1525.H78 2000
    372.4—dc21   00-059776

Editor: Lois Bridges
Production service: Patricia Adams
Production coordination: Renée Le Verrier
Cover photography: Bob Welsh/Moments in Time Photography
Cover design: Darci Mehall/Aureo Design
Manufacturing: Louise Richardson

Printed in the United States of America on acid-free paper
04 03 02   ML   4 5

To Brenden, Megan, and Kyle
    You make everything special.

To Stephen
    My partner, friend, and encourager—

I love you.

Contents

· ·

Contents

Acknowledgments

· ·

The children have taught me so much. They are the ones who lead the way and show me the next steps. The teachers of the Beaverton School District are my family, my coaches, and my mentors. The teachers across the country I have been honored to meet in my seminars are also part of the fabric of this book. The teachers ask the questions that help our profession to grow and to constantly reach for higher levels of proficiency in meeting the needs of the learners we serve.

In particular, I would like to acknowledge the following individuals. Patty Noel, my friend and enthusiastic flag bearer. Theresa Therriault, Judy Hjelseth, and Bev Hobson had the courage to believe and to help make a far-fetched vision a reality for teachers and children. Jodi Wilson, literacy consultant and master teacher from Coeur d'Alene, Idaho, brings new richness to my vision of teaching and learning. Robin Case, Ginny Kopacz, and Mei-Ling Shiroishi celebrate children in the most positive of ways and kindly allowed me to participate in their literacy learning families. Frank Koontz, Rich Herzberg, and Kathie Foreman, Bureau of Education and Research—they gave me wings.

Kevlynn Annandale, Manager of Consultants for First Steps, USA/Heinemann. She made me jump off the bridge and Lois Bridges, my editor, held out the safety net. I will always be grateful. Renée Le Verrier and Patty Adams taught me about the power of active listening and attention to detail. They understood my goals and helped make them real.

I especially thank my family. My husband, Steve, and my three children cooked, cleaned, took care of the house, and offered me endless encouragement and support. My eldest son, Brenden, wrote much of the poetry encompassed in these minilessons.

1

Getting Started with Minilessons

Why Teach Minilessons?

In an age of overloaded curricula, tight school schedules, and the recent research on the brain, minilessons make good sense. They provide intense, direct instruction in a skill or understanding that children will use immediately after the moment of instruction. They are focused and strategic. The goal is to:

> Teach a small, learnable amount. Practice it in real contexts. Talk about what you learned and how it worked. The minilesson is about narrowing the field of vision so that you can truly see a fine point. Study it. Then, use the new understanding in a real and meaningful way.

Minilessons capture interest without risking boredom. They are grounded in immediate practice and need. They allow teachers to flexibly cover important topics while fitting into any instructional paradigm and organizational structure.

Snapshots Is About Minilessons for Literacy

The idea is to:

- Integrate minilessons across the rich literacy opportunities of the entire curriculum.
- Make the most of even short segments of time.
- Show, more than tell, how to use the learning.
- Provide immediate practice for the learning in real meaningful contexts.
- Discuss what was learned and how it can be applied.

Show Them What You Want Them to Do

In every snapshot in this book, it is expected that you, the teacher, will provide strategy lessons using real books or transparencies on the overhead projector. It is essential to *show* the students what is in your head by modeling or demonstrating. The goal is make your thought processes as transparent as possible by talking about your thinking, talking about your decisions, talking about how the strategy works and how you will use it.

Provide Guided Practice

After you model and explain the strategy, students need time for guided practice. This is a time when you can coach and support their attempts to apply what they have learned. This is the time to offer a lot of support, observe closely, and repeat your explanations for students who do not seem to understand. After this supported or guided practice, the students need a time to engage in independent use of the strategy.

Move Toward Independent Practice

Independent practice occurs when students read real books and write real messages independently using the target learning. Their personal goal is to attempt to use the learning independently within the context of a real literacy task.

Allow for Reflection

The last step is time for reflection, time to talk about what was learned, and how well the strategy worked. As you read the snapshots that follow, you will notice Key Questions have been included to support the reflections of your students. These Key Questions are discussion starters to encourage reflection and assist your learners in considering long-term use of the strategies they are learning.

The Process

Minilessons are based on a gradual release of responsibility (Pearson and Fielding, 1991). The teacher starts with all of the responsibility and shows, not tells, the students how to engage in the target understanding. Guided practice is next as the learners, with teacher support, approximate the behaviors while the teacher is there to assist and coach. Lastly, the students show their understanding independently during authentic reading and writing opportunities. At the beginning of the process, the students are observers and the teacher carries the full responsibility. During guided practice, students and the teacher *share* the responsibility. Students attempt to use the learning and the teacher is actively coaching as a partner in the process. In the final stage of independent practice, the

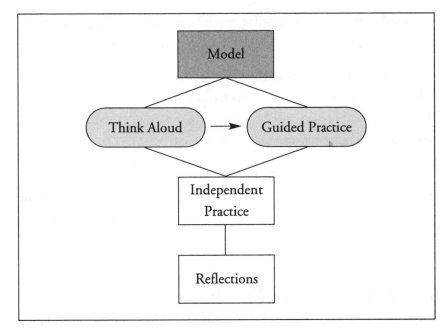

FIGURE 1.1 Teacher involvement is shaded; it lessens through the process.

students carry the full responsibility for use of the strategy. The teacher is now free to observe, assess, and determine the level of understanding.

Introduce the Topic/Strategy

Explain the goal to your students. Tell them what they will learn.

Model the Use of the Strategy

Talk out loud about what you are doing. Tell the students what you are thinking. Explain why you are doing what you are doing and how you decide when or if to use the strategy. The goal is to make your thinking as transparent as possible so the students will understand how to use and apply the learning. This is the most important part of the minilesson. Think of this as the picture that appears on the front of a jigsaw puzzle box. The picture gives you a really clear understanding of how the little pieces of the puzzle fit together. The goal of your demonstration is to provide your students with this clear picture of the strategy itself, of the thinking processes you use to apply the strategy, and of the decisions that go into deciding when to use the strategy.

Provide Guided Practice

Work with your students to practice the strategy. This is often a good time for partners, cooperative groups, or teams to work together and support each other while you act as a coach, praising appropriate use of the strategy and assisting those who need additional help. This is also a good time to assess how well your students understood your demonstration. Those who understood the demonstration and are using the strategy can move directly into independent practice. Those who seem confused or lacking in confidence might benefit from having you repeat the minilesson for them as individuals or in a small group.

Offer Independent Practice

Children work independently using the strategy in their personal work. This is a second opportunity to assess understanding, support appropriate uses of the learning, and reteach as needed.

Encourage Self-Reflection

Students now have a chance to stop and consider: What did we just learn (the content)? How did the strategy work for us (the process)? How else might we use the strategy?

Keeping Track of Minilessons

I like to keep a written list or log of minilessons. I list minilessons I have done in reading, writing, the content areas, and classroom management. I also have a system so I can note when I repeat a minilesson. This list allows me to monitor my minilessons over time so I can be reflective about my teaching. My goal is to be sure that I am demonstrating the full range of literacy understandings that are appropriate to the age of my learners. For example, my log of minilessons might help me to notice that I have demonstrated the sound symbol relationship for the letter *m* six times but I have not worked on the letter *w*. It might help me to notice that I am continually reminding individuals about spaces between words but I have not done a minilesson for the whole class.

Sample Phonics Minilesson Log

Date	Minilesson Taught	Book or Overhead Used	Reteach Dates
10/3	*-ed* endings	*Three Billy Goats Gruff*	10/30, 11/15
10/4	words with *or*	*More, More, More*	
10/5	*-ing* words	*The Jigaree*	10/7

Sample Procedure Minilesson Log

Date	Minilesson Taught	Book or Overhead Used	Reteach Dates
9/5	Using a writing folder	Sample writing folder	
9/6	Using the word wall in writing	Word wall	9/10
9/7	What to do when you finish a piece of writing	List of writers workshop options	

Sample Content Area Minilesson Log

Date	Minilesson Taught	Book or Overhead Used	Reteach Dates
12/1	Using pictures to predict in science text	Science textbook, p. 32	12/10
12/2	Using boldfaced text	Social Studies book, p. 16	
12/3	Reading captions	Science text, p. 35	

Planning Future Minilessons

I keep a list of minilessons that I want to teach. This becomes a rich collection to draw from on a daily basis. I create the list and keep it going by observing my students. With these observations I can ensure that I am targeting my teaching directly to learner need. I also use this list to remind myself to emphasize strategies for the challenges I know the children are about to face. For example, I could use this log to remind myself of the range of test-taking strategies I want to emphasize during the two months before the standardized test is taking place.

Minilessons to Teach

Topics	Comments	Date Presented
Capital letters for pronouns	Alex, Sylda, Hector	10/22 G. Reading
		10/23 Writers Workshop
Previewing before reading	Whole class	10/30 Readers Workshop
	Ask Ron to help demonstrate	10/31 G. Reading
		11/2 Lit. Circle for Anna and group
Organizing writing supplies	Manuel, Simi, Paul	
Bubbling in answer sheets	Whole class	
Finding answers in passages	Whole class	
Timing yourself on the test	Juan's group	

Using Student Work Samples

I am constantly watching for samples of student work that will help me present minilessons. When I see a student who has mastered putting spaces between words, for example, I might ask that student for permission to make a transparency of his work, show it on the overhead, and then use it to teach a minilesson on spacing.

On another day, I might notice that a student has really mastered previewing pictures and reading captions before attempting to read the science text. That student could then be asked to help me do the minilesson using a big book or a transparency created from a page in the science book.

I find that students love to have their work displayed on the overhead as well as to tell each other about strategies that they have found to be personally helpful.

While it is ideal to use current work samples from class, it can also be helpful to keep a file folder filled with student work samples and add to it continuously so that you have a quick resource for transparencies.

Varying Your Minilessons

You might consider asking yourself how minilessons might fit into instructional times such as:

- Independent reading: when students read independently in books they have selected themselves
- Shared book experiences: when you use a big book or an overhead transparency to teach specific understandings about print
- Guided reading: when you work with a small group of students to support their reading of a book that you have selected for them
- Literature discussions: when you invite groups of students to meet and talk in depth about their reading
- Textbooks: when students need to understand more as they read in science, social studies, and health texts

How might minilessons be woven into whole-class experiences as well as small groups?

If you begin to think of minilessons as part of the fabric of your instruction and consider them a natural opening to each instructional activity, they can become a staple in your instructional tool kit.

Small Segments of Time

It is ideal to connect minilessons to guided practice and independence. But, the educational day is often laden with small segments of time that at first glance appear useless: the ten-minute window between the visit from the City Councilman and P.E. or the seven minutes you suddenly gained when a project was finished early. These are key moments that could be opportunities for minilessons. Deliberate, purposeful, intentional teaching in a short period of time can turn those seemingly useless moments into high-impact teaching/learning opportunities. When I use minilessons in this way, I try to make them fun and interesting, then make a pledge to myself and the students that guided practice and independent practice will occur at a later time.

Minilesson Topics

The possibilities are endless. The following list is to spark your thinking:

PROCEDURAL MINILESSONS

Where to sit during reading time

How to be a good listener during sharing

How to give a book talk

Monitoring noise during reading time

What to do when you finish a book

Kinds of questions to ask during a book share

What to do during small group reading time

Getting ready for a reading conference

Taking care of books

Rules of readers workshop

Getting along in writers workshop

Peer conferencing

Your reading folder

How to read aloud

How to use the listening center

STRATEGIES/SKILLS

How to choose good books

Selection of topics for your learning log

Connecting reading to your life

Using sticky notes while reading

Using context with unknown words

Monitoring comprehension

Self-correcting

Making predictions

Using letters and word parts

Directionality of print

Sound-symbol relationships

Phonemic awareness

Story mapping

Retelling a story

Making inferences

Fact and opinion

Determining key ideas

Using prior knowledge

Asking questions before/during/after reading

EXPOSITORY

Locating information

Using captions under pictures

Dealing with content specific vocabulary

Note taking

Skim and scan

Using pictures/graphs/charts

Using the questions at the end of the chapter

Using the contents and index

Structures for expository texts

Textbooks

LITERARY

Fiction structures	Foreshadowing
Figurative language	Personification
Books that show emotion	Alliteration
Mood/theme	Poetry
Author studies	Endings
Quotations	Illustrations
Setting	Character development
Genre	Point of view
Leads	
Retells	

The snapshots that follow are demonstrations of possible minilessons. The best ones will be those that evolve naturally as you observe your students, see their unique areas of need, and then lead them forward into the world of strategic literacy.

2

Reading Strategies Alive!
Knowing What to Do and When to Do It

*P*roficient readers are strategic. They monitor their comprehension during reading. They notice when they do or do
not understand. They can identify confusing ideas and words, then implement strategies to help themselves deal with the problem. Proficient readers
also shift their reading style and speed to meet their purpose (Keene and Zimmerman, 1997; Pearson et al., 1992). Most of all, proficient readers have a
rich collection of strategies to draw from as they interact with the varying
texts of our world.

Developing a Strategic Stance

In many ways, this is similar to the operating style of an effective parent
or teacher. Effective parents and teachers respond to their different children in different ways, and shift those responses even further in response
to individual mood swings. One style of response doesn't fit all children
at all times. The same is true of reading. Readers need tool belts that are
laden with a variety of strategies and a strong inner sense of empowerment with those tools. An effective reader knows that when one thing
doesn't work, you shift strategies and try something else. A good reader
identifies which strategies work for each kind of text, and understands
that the goal is always to create meaning while reading. For example,
when I read a novel I start at page one and let myself savor the joy of
reading page after page, in order. When reading a recipe, I start with the
list of ingredients, slide to the oven temperature and the number of serv-
ings, then move in and out of the directions as I assemble the recipe. In
my computer manual, I read as little as possible. I use the index and the

table of contents to search for answers to explicit questions and then quickly close the book.

Each kind of reading demands a different set of strategies. My job as a reader is to know which strategies to use in each kind of text.

To support learners in developing this strategic stance, it is critical to give them time to observe proficient readers applying, using, and sometimes discarding strategies as they are tested. It is also critical to give them an opportunity to be reflective about their use of strategies so that they might consider which strategies to use in which contexts and which ones are most personally meaningful.

I believe that the best strategy lists are those developed by students. To support this reflective thinking, I like to provide opportunities for students to develop class strategy lists and personal strategy logs. These logs might take the form of a chart on the wall, a bookmark, or a simple list. The important issue is to keep the lists active by constantly reviewing them to add newly discovered strategies and delete those that may be less useful than originally anticipated. You can use minilessons to support strategy development by introducing a new strategy, showing how to use a strategy in multiple contexts, or as a way to demonstrate additional strategies that might expand students' lists of good reader strategies.

The following list of good reader strategies is not meant to be all-encompassing, but rather a springboard from which your minilessons and strategy reflections might evolve.

Good Reader Strategies

Before Reading
- Preview the book:
    Is this fiction or nonfiction?
    Preview pictures, charts, graphs
    Preview any boldfaced type or headings
- Activate prior knowledge about the topic and the genre
- Understand the task
- Set a purpose for reading
- Think about which strategies might work best in this kind of text

During Reading
- Confirm or adjust predictions
- Adjusts reading to match the kind of text
- Monitor comprehension: Does this make sense?
- Apply fix-up strategies when there is confusion
    Re-read
    Read on to search for more information
    Look at word parts: Beginning and ending sounds
    Look for little words in bigger words
    Put in another word that makes sense
- Use context
- Use text structure
- Skim and scan to find answers to questions
- Stop frequently to reflect on what has been read so far
- Visualize
- Identify important ideas
- Make inferences, conclusions, evaluations, interpretations

After Reading
- Reflect:
    What did I learn?
    How is this important?
    What strategies worked well in this text?
- Summarize
- Synthesize: Pull it all together in your head

© 2000 by Linda Hoyt from *Snapshots*. Portsmouth, NH: Heinemann.

I Am a Good Reader

Before Reading I Think About . . .
- the title
- the pictures
- what I already know about the topic
- my purpose for reading
- my predictions about the text
- my questions

While I am Reading I . . .
- ask myself, Does this make sense?
- ask myself, Does this sound right?
- focus on beginning sounds, "chunks" within words, and endings to figure out unknown words
- backtrack when the meaning isn't clear
- read on past difficult words or groups of words to get more information
- confirm or correct my predictions

After Reading I . . .
- think about the author's message
- reflect on how the text matched or didn't match my predictions
- think about how the text relates to real life

© 2000 by Linda Hoyt from *Snapshots*. Portsmouth, NH: Heinemann.

Personal Strategy List

I like to start with an overhead transparency of a text or a big book with large pictures. I then begin to think out loud and explicitly describe my thinking as I approach the text. I explain how I look at the page as a whole and decide if it is fiction or nonfiction. I also point out that I am going to look at the pictures and the title to help myself understand what the passage will be about and to set a personal purpose for reading. If it is a passage on sharks for example, my think aloud might sound something like:

> *This page has a large photograph of a shark and the words are in boxes arranged around the picture so I predict this will be an information text, not a story.*
>
> *I see that there is a smaller picture of a shark's mouth showing its teeth. This makes me think of the time that I got to go to Sea World and see real sharks. They had rows and rows of teeth and they looked really mean. I remember that a guide at Sea World told us that not all sharks are dangerous to people.*
>
> *I also remember that sharks need to keep moving to be able to breathe. I think I read that in a book once.*
>
> *As I look at this page, I wonder if it will tell about what sharks eat and where they live. Those are things I would really like to know.*

I modify the number of strategies in my think aloud to match the developmental level and amount of strategic reading experience represented in the group. For an emergent group, I stop my think aloud after only one or two strategies. With a group experienced in strategy conversations, I continue beyond the sample above and integrate some think aloud conversations into an oral reading of the text.

The next step is to show the students how to record the strategies I have used on a personal strategy log. I explain to the students that I am going to stop and list any strategies I have used so far and then record them on my list. To ensure that students can observe your writing and thinking, you could make an overhead transparency of the Strategy Log or list your strategies on chart paper. As each strategy is added to the log, I ask the students to help me decide if it is a strategy that could be used again in another book and be worthy of adding to our class strategy list.

Sample: Personal Reading Strategies List

Reader: <u>Mrs. Hoyt</u>   Date list started <u>9/25</u>

My reading strategies:	Reflection: Is it working? Have you used the strategy in more than one book?
<u>Look at pictures</u>	_____
<u>Ask: Is it fact or fiction?</u>	_____
<u>What do I know about this topic?</u>	_____
<u>What do I hope to learn?</u>	_____

The students are now ready to select books and personally follow the steps. This process works best when students have multiple opportunities to follow the steps with narrative as well as nonfiction. Then they continue to reflect on how the strategies are working and with which texts they work best. The second column in the Personal Strategy Log is designed to provide students with a place to record their ongoing research and reflections.

The goal is to initiate a log that will be ongoing over time and to emphasize that good readers have many strategies from which to choose. The key is to be flexible and ready to try different strategies when a particular one doesn't work.

Key Questions
- Which strategies help you understand?
- Which strategies work with which books?

Personal Reading Strategies List

Reader _____   Date list started _____

My reading strategies:

Reflection: Is it working? Have you used the strategy in more than one book? Does it seem to work best with one kind of text?

_____

_____

_____

_____

_____

_____

_____

_____

_____

_____

© 2000 by Linda Hoyt from *Snapshots*. Portsmouth, NH: Heinemann.

"I Wonder" Questions

Good readers engage in self-questioning before, during, and after reading to monitor their own comprehension and to integrate readings with prior knowledge (Cooper, 1993). To assist children in utilizing the natural questions that are inherent when their curiosity is aroused, I provide many minilessons on self-questioning. I find that the phrase, "I Wonder . . . ," provides structure for the questions that flow naturally through before, during, and after reading reflections.

For this snapshot, I select a book unknown to the children. This can be a high-quality picture book with a problem/solution structure or a big book. Fiction and nonfiction work equally well.

It is helpful to have chart paper or an overhead transparency of the following page so you can record the student's questions.

After demonstrating the process of gathering "I Wonder" questions, I ask the students to personally engage in the process by listing "I Wonder" questions before, during, and after reading and then talking about how it influenced their reading.

This would be a perfect time for the children to return to their Personal Strategy Logs to see if "I Wonder" is a strategy they want to add to either the class list of reading strategies or to their personal logs.

To provide ongoing support for this strategy, I try to build in stop points for "I Wonder" questions during shared book experience, guided reading, and independent reading. During shared book and guided reading, I can provide the stop points as I guide students through the text. For independent reading, I have found it helpful to provide two or three sticky notes and ask the students to put markers into their books with the understanding that when they come to a sticky note while reading independently, it is their job to stop reading and generate at least one "I Wonder" question. Some children seem to benefit from taking time to write their questions, others employ the strategy easily by just thinking about the "I Wonder" questions and then quickly returning to their reading.

Key Questions
- What do you wonder about?
- What do you want to know?
- What do you hope the author will communicate?
- Are you making connections to what you know about the world, about other books?
- Are you making connections between your personal experiences and this text?

"I Wonder . . ."

Before Reading
(Look at the cover of the book and think of ways to complete this stem:)

I Wonder _____

I Wonder _____

I Wonder _____

During Reading
(Stop at least twice during reading to generate more "I Wonder" statements.)

I Wonder _____

I Wonder _____

I Wonder _____

After Reading
(Provide time to reflect on the text and then consider additional "I Wonder" statements that might reflect the content and/or the author's craft.)

I Wonder _____

I Wonder _____

I Wonder _____

© 2000 by Linda Hoyt from *Snapshots*. Portsmouth, NH: Heinemann.

Fix It! Bookmarks

Good readers use a variety of strategies to determine unknown words. They might:

- look at the pictures and think about what is happening on the page
- read on for more information and then return to the difficult word
- reread the sentence/paragraph and come through again
- use the beginning and ending sounds of a word
- chunk the word
- sound it out
- think of another word that makes sense then read on to see if it makes sense

To ensure that all of these strategies are included in each reader's repertoire, you might plan minilessons focused on each individual strategy then continue to remind your students about strategy use during shared book experience, guided reading, and independent reading.

The first challenge is to help students develop an awareness of the full range of strategies for dealing with unknown words. I like to use cloze activities to heighten this awareness combined with the development of Fix It! bookmarks. Cloze activities provide children with a text from which key words have been omitted. In a big book or on an overhead transparency, I cover words with brightly colored pieces of sticky notes then ask the students to think of words that would make sense before moving the sticky note and exposing the covered word.

The first Fix It! bookmark on the following page is an example of a prepared bookmark that could be photocopied and used in guided reading, literature circles, and independent reading. The second Fix It! Bookmark is much like the Personal Reading Strategy List shown earlier in this chapter and is designed to be developed by students as they work with various strategies. The key issue is to focus reader attention on reading strategies in *all* the texts they encounter, then provide continual and ongoing support so that the strategies will be fully implemented and incorporated into their personal collection of good reader options.

Minilesson Ideas

- Independent reading: Ask each student to focus on one strategy from their bookmark and consciously think about that strategy during Sustained Silent Reading (SSR). At the end of the session, have partners tell each other which strategy they used and how it worked for them.

- Guided reading: After the picture walk, use a small wipe-off board to demonstrate how to find little words in big words then invite the students to try the strategy on words they encounter when they independently read their guided reading book. At the end of guided reading, invite them to talk about how it worked and put a mark next to "Chunk the word" on their personal bookmarks if they think the strategy is a good one for them.

- Shared book: During shared book experience, provide each student with a bookmark. At a predictable point in the text, stop on a word and ask the students to suggest a strategy to try. You might even try several strategies to demonstrate how each might assist a reader.

Key Questions

- Have you challenged yourself to try a new strategy?
- How will you modify your bookmark when you think of a new strategy to add?

Fix It! Bookmark Templates

Fix It! Bookmark
I am a good reader. I can:

Ask: Does this make sense?

Does it sound right?

Look at the picture

Backtrack

Read on

Look at the first and last letter

Sound it out

Look at parts of the word

Use another word that makes sense

I also can:

_____

_____

_____

_____

Fix It! Bookmark
I am a good reader. I can:

_____

_____

_____

_____

_____

_____

_____

_____

_____

_____

_____

_____

© 2000 by Linda Hoyt from *Snapshots*. Portsmouth, NH: Heinemann.

Strategy Cards

Strategy cards provide a variation on the format of the Fix It! Bookmark. When using these cards, I provide a set for each student to keep in an envelope and encourage them to keep the envelope where it is readily available for reading opportunities. I also place strategy cards on notebook rings and place them in literacy centers, the classroom library, and other key points in the classroom so the students are reminded to use them.

For minilessons, I keep a set of enlarged strategy cards at the front of the room so I can use them during large- and small-group demonstrations.

Sample Minilesson

Place an enlarged set of strategy cards in a very visible place such as the chalk tray, in a pocket chart, or taped to the chalkboard. Review the cards and the strategies they represent.

Make an overhead transparency of a poem or select a favorite picture book. In the middle of reading, stop once or twice and ask the students to recommend one strategy you might try with an unknown word. Do not stop too often or discuss the strategies in depth during the reading as this may cause the students to forget the storyline.

At the end of reading, you can go back and reflect on the strategies tried, how they worked, and how the students might be able to use them personally.

Other Possibilities

- During independent reading, ask the students to arrange their strategy cards on the desk so that they are all visible. If a card is used, ask the reader to move it to a designated place on their desk and be ready to talk about it at the end of independent reading.
- Invite students to examine a narrative and a nonfiction text and talk about which strategy cards might be most useful with each kind of text.
- During partner reading, have readers lay the strategy cards on their desks and consciously try to notice if their partner used any of the strategies on the cards. Have them tell their partners what they noticed. Was one strategy used all the time? Were several strategies tried?

- Have students make their own strategy cards. They might ask: If a friend asked you for help with reading, what advice would you give them?

Key Questions

- How might you teach your parents or another student about these strategies and the ways in which they assist your reading?

FIGURE 2.1 Strategy posters in the first-grade classroom of Susan Morrell-Dunsky, William Walker Elementary, Beaverton, Oregon.

Strategy Card Templates

THINK ABOUT THE STORY

LOOK AT THE PICTURE

BACKTRACK

READ ON

USE THE BEGINNING AND
ENDING SOUNDS
What would make sense and
have that beginning or ending
sound?

CHUNK THE WORD
What would make sense and
have these word parts? Are
there any little words?

COVER THE UNKNOWN WORD
WITH YOUR FINGER AND
THINK ABOUT WHAT WOULD
SOUND RIGHT

USE WHAT YOU KNOW ABOUT
THE TOPIC

© 2000 by Linda Hoyt from *Snapshots*. Portsmouth, NH: Heinemann.

Cloze in Big and Little Books

While the inventor of sticky notes may not have had children in mind, they are a wonderful educational tool and can be especially helpful for supporting reading strategies through cloze activities. I like to use sticky notes to cover words in big books, words on the overhead, or words in guided reading books. This gives the students an opportunity to utilize a range of good reader strategies that include but are not limited to visual information.

Examples in a Big Book

- Cover predictable words with two layers of sticky note paper so the shadow of the bold print doesn't show through and ask the students to try to determine which word is hiding. After they make their predictions, ask them to think of the beginning sound that should appear for their word. If they guess *yelled*, they would identify "Y" as the beginning sound.

    "Who's that walking on my bridge?" [   ] the troll.

Then, slide the sticky note to the side to uncover just the beginning sound.

    "Who's that walking on my bridge?" g[   ] the troll.

You might ask the students, "Do you still think the word is *yelled*? Now that you can see the beginning sound, what do you think the word might be?" and continue working your way through the phonemes in the word as you slide the sticky note across the letters.

- Use two colors of sticky notes to help the children separate onsets and rimes as a natural extension of using good reader strategies. Use one color over the onset and the other over the rime.

    "Who's that walking on my bridge?" [████][   ] the troll.

    "Who's that walking on my bridge?" gr[████] the troll.

As the students predict the hidden word, you can remove the first sticky note that is over the onset (the part of the word before the vowel) and then later remove the second color sticky note that is over the rime (the vowel and the rest of the word).

- Cover all of the word except for the beginning sound. When they get really good, you can cover several words in the same sentence.

  "Who's that w_____ on my b_____?" g_____ the troll.

Examples in Guided Reading
- Cover key words in the text to encourage strategy use and engage the children in a conversation about both the predicted words and the strategies used.
- Have students "surprise" one another by covering up two or three words in a familiar guided reading book and then trying to guess which word is hiding.

Cloze on the Overhead

Make a transparency of a poem such as the one following and cover key words with sticky notes. Invite your students to talk about the strategies they use to determine the hidden words. You may want to experiment by covering rhyming words, parts of speech, word endings, words that start with a particular letter to support your focus strategies. Again, when the students predict the covered words, ask them to also predict the sounds and phonemes so you can uncover the words a bit at a time.

Key Questions
- How might you use the strategy of predicting words and letters when you are reading independently?
- How can you help yourself remember to do this?
- Have you ever tried using your finger to cover a tricky word and then thinking really hard about what would make sense, just like in the minilesson?

HOMEWORK

Math
Reading
Spelling
What else will they send?

English
Science
Social Studies
Will it ever end?

My TV time is history
My body's growing weak
I need to run and jump about
Not warm this chair all week

My father says, "Come on let's play!
I've got your baseball mitt."
But I have to sadly shake my head . . .
This homework is a pit!

© 2000 by Linda Hoyt from *Snapshots*. Portsmouth, NH: Heinemann.

Predicting Letters and Words

Good readers can move through text rapidly and smoothly because they are continually using their knowledge of the world, their knowledge of language, and their knowledge of print (Clay, 1998). When this integrated use of cueing systems (meaning, structure, visual) is combined with a sense of place and use for the text (pragmatic system), the result is fluent, strategic reading. The meaning cues are used as a reader thinks about what makes sense, about how the world works, and activates prior knowledge. The structural cues are our sense of how the English language goes together. We expect certain kinds of words to occur in certain places, for fairy tales to open with "Once upon a time . . . ," and for our reading to sound the same as people talk. The visual cues are the print on the page, the sounds and symbols, the shapes of words, the placement of pictures and print, etc. The pragmatic system relates to the context. We expect a computer manual to sound different from a recipe. We expect the language of a poem to be structured differently than the newspaper. The pragmatic system helps us to connect purpose and place just as we subtly adjust the way we speak when crooning to a baby, making a formal presentation, or chatting with a friend.

Bringing It Together

To me, it is an awesome moment when these systems come together for children. There is a light that dawns in their eyes and a sense of empowerment that makes the world of print a place of confident exploration.

I do notice, however, that the integration of these systems is sometimes subconscious for learners. This concerns me because a learner who is subconsciously using strategies won't be as likely to know which strategies are helpful and should be retained as compared to those strategies that are really counterproductive and should be discarded.

I have interviewed many parents of those miraculous five-year-olds who come to school reading and they tell me that no one taught them, it just happened! I wonder how heightening conscious awareness of reading strategies might help those self-starters move even further along.

I have also interviewed those out of balance readers who have been explicitly taught to use one or more of the systems but can't seem to pull them into coordinated use. For both kinds of learners, activities that enable them to sample from the visual information and consciously apply semantic and syntactic knowledge, can bring a *conscious awareness* of what happens during reading.

I always accompany these explorations of text with lots of conversation and questions such as: How do you know? What makes you think so? What letters do you think should be there?

Key Questions

- What does a good reader do that makes it possible to predict words and letters even when you can't see them on the page?
- How might you do this when you are reading by yourself?
- What strategies might we add to our class or personal strategy lists?

Cloze Activities

Once upon a time there were three billy goats who lived on a mountainside. There was a very small billy ___ ___ ___ ___ named Little Billy Goat Gruff. There was a m__ ___ ___ __ __ sized billy goat named Middle Billy Goat Gruff. There was a great ___ ___ ___ billy goat everyone called Big Billy Goat Gruff.

One ___ ___ ___ , the three ___ ___ ___ ___ ___ goats were hungry so they decided to go up the ___ ___ ___ ___ and eat some green ___ ___ ___ ___ ___ . To get to the hill, they had to ___ ___ ___ ___ ___ a bridge which crossed over a r___ ___ ___ ___ .

Little Billy ___ ___ ___ ___ G___ ___ ___ ___ was really h___ ___ ___ ___ ___ so he ___ ___ ___ across the bridge fir___ ___ . Middle Billy Goat Gruff was the n___ ___ ___ to cr___ ___ ___ the br__ ___ ___ ___ . He was so ___ ___g that his feet ___ ___ ___ ___ a lot of noise when he walked ___ ___ ___ ___ ___ ___ the bridge.

Just as he reached the end of the bridge, a tr___ ___ ___ jumped up and sc___ ___ ___ ___ him!

Strategy Reflection

© 2000 by Linda Hoyt from *Snapshots*. Portsmouth, NH: Heinemann.

Morning Message

Many teachers create daily opportunities for this kind of strategy integration by having a morning message waiting on the overhead projector or the chalkboard each day when the students enter the class. The morning message might tell about coming events, remind students of upcoming class activities, or cue up the students' thinking on important reading strategies.

Additional Cloze Samples to Use as Transparencies

Good Morning!

Today is a special ___ ___ ___. We are going to have a Read In and we will get to ___ ___ ___ ___ all day. I hope you remembered to br__ ___ ___ your favorite ___ ___ ___ ___ ___ . This is a wonderful time to relax, read, and talk about the books we all enjoy the most. For another treat, we __ ___ ___ ___ have a guest. The principal is going to ___ ___ ___ ___ her favorite picture ___ ___ ___ ___ and share it with ___ ___.

Sincerely,

Mrs. Hoyt

Good M___ ___ ___ ___ ___ ___,

Today as you st___ ___ ___ your read__ ___ ___ workshop, please remember to ___ ___ ___ ___ quietly. Please also re__ ___ ___ ___ ___ ___ to pre___ ___ ___ ___ while you read. When you __ ___ ___ ___ ___ ___ ___, you are more likely to remember ___ ___ ___ ___ you read and to enjoy ___ ___ ___ ___ ___ ___ ___ you have chosen. Have __ n__ __ __ __ ___ ___.

Sincere__ ___,

Mrs. H___ ___ ___

Strategy Reflection

© 2000 by Linda Hoyt from *Snapshots*. Portsmouth, NH: Heinemann.

Reviewing My Own Strategies

The Demonstration

You will need a transparency, big book, or individual student copies of a text and an audiotape of you reading that text. For the sake of the demonstration, it would be helpful if your audiotape includes an opening in which you think aloud about the topic to make connections to your prior knowledge and your personal questions, and at least two additional examples of you using good reader strategies in your reading.

Explain to the students that you have made a tape of yourself reading aloud and that you want them to identify the good reader strategies you remembered to use.

Before listening to the tape, review with the students a class chart of good reader strategies, the Reading Strategy Cards, or Fix It bookmarks.

Then, have the students follow along as they listen to you read. I always tell the students that their goal is to notice your reading strategies and be ready to talk about them. (They need to see the text as they listen, so be sure to use a visual of the print.)

Stop the tape periodically and ask what they noticed. Did they see any good reader strategies in action? List their observations on a chart such as the sample overhead transparency on the following page.

Guided/Independent Practice

Provide each student with a copy of the Personal Monitoring Log on the following page and an opportunity to read into a tape recorder. The goal is to read and make a recording then rewind the tape and listen to themselves as they follow along in the original text. This is a highly personal experience. Each student reads into the tape recorder alone and listens either alone or with a teacher/coach. When the student notices that a good reader strategy has been used, the tape recorder is stopped so the strategy used can be recorded on the log. For emergent readers and readers without previous experience with strategy instruction, it is helpful to focus on one strategy such as "backtracking to regain momentum." For more experienced readers, a wider range of strategic behaviors may be monitored.

Postreading conferences can be held in groups or individually to give students an opportunity to talk about their strategies and their personal strategy goals.

Key Questions
- Do you think your strategy list is growing? Do you notice yourself using more strategies than before?
- Are you using all of the strategies that you could? Are there any you could add or use more often?

Personal Monitoring Log

Name _____   Date _____

Name of Story _____

Directions

1. Select the reading strategies you will be listening for in this reading.

Activate Prior Knowledge	I Wonder Questions	Read On	Backtrack	Beginning Sounds
Ending Sounds	Chunking	Meaningful Substitution	Other_____	

2. Read into a tape recorder and try to use the strategies you have selected.

3. Rewind the tape and listen to yourself read. The goal is to track under the lines of print and STOP the tape recorder when you notice that you have used the strategy. Make a tally mark in the appropriate box to show you have used the strategy.

4. Meet with your teacher and/or your group to talk about the strategies you used and your goals for continued reading.

© 2000 by Linda Hoyt from *Snapshots*. Portsmouth, NH: Heinemann.

Strategy Poem

Read the poem that follows and assess it. Which strategies are missing?

I Am Learning To Read

I am learning to read and it's lots of fun
I can read from pictures and I feel like I've won
Then I look at the words and I try to make sense
But the rules don't work and I feel like I'm dense

I read SO and GO and NO and THROW
This is kind of fun
When I keep it up and try for TO . . .
Now, I feel like I'm kinda dumb

My teacher says that strategies are what I need to read:
I get a picture in my head
I backtrack to reread
I sound it out all by myself
And ask: Does this make sense?
I even read on to learn some more
And now I **Really Read!**

© 2000 by Linda Hoyt from *Snapshots*. Portsmouth, NH: Heinemann.

Vocabulary Replacement

When readers come to an unknown word and the strategies listed earlier in this chapter still don't help, they may want to consider substituting a meaningful word to enable them to continue reading and still make meaning.

The following snapshot could be made into an overhead transparency or photocopied so that students could have a shared reading experience and discuss not only the words that might make sense, but the strategies they employ to enable themselves to continue meaningfully through the rest of the passage.

You will note that the margins have been enlarged to allow for note taking in the margin to the right. These notes could be collected during or after reading, depending on the age and learning style of your students.

After reading, discussing, and noting the strategies that were used, students could return to their class strategy lists, Personal Strategy Logs or Fix It! bookmarks to consider possible strategy additions.

Key Questions to Consider After Reading
- Did you understand the story in spite of the nonsense words?
- What does that tell you about dealing with words you don't know?
- What strategies helped you to get the meaning?
- Which strategies might help you in other texts?
- Are there any strategies we need to add to our class strategy list or your personal strategy lists?

Key Questions for Teachers
- Are you remembering to do lots of think alouds to help students see strategies in action?

In the next snapshot it may help to stop after the first paragraph . . . think aloud . . . and demonstrate how you deal with confusion before inviting the students to read and express their observations.

The Three Billy Goats Gruff

Once upon a time there were three billy goats named Gruff. One billy goat was quite small and was named Little Billy Goat Gruff. One billy goat was large sized and was named Big Billy Goat Gruff. The third billy goat was enormous and everyone simply called him BIG.

One day the three billy goats were hungry and decided to go to the norploex where the grass was green and lush. To get there they had to go over a bridge that was so fargoal, they could only cross one at a time.

The Little Billy Goat Gruff ran fegsmer across the bridge and was soon eating the lush, green grass. Big Billy Goat Gruff moved more mednes so he took a while to get across the bridge. Just as he reached the end of the bridge, a nasty old troll hopped in front of him and elexed, "Stop, Big Billy Goat! Nobody crosses my bridge without paying the toll."

Big Billy Goat was so surprised that he just stood there with his abreech open. BIG, however, was watching and quietly valnoxed under the bridge and came up behind the nasty old troll. With one swing of his mighty formot, BIG knocked that old troll off the bridge and into the water. The nasty, old troll was so scared that he ran home sneeling and was never heard from again.

Group Think Aloud/Activating Prior Knowledge

The prior knowledge a reader brings to a text has an enormous influence on understanding (Pearson and Fielding, 1991; Cooper, 1993, Keene and Zimmerman, 1997). This prior knowledge or schema is our frame of reference for developing understanding and creating meaning from text.

Please read the following:

> Coordinate geometry can be used to measure the slope of lines. Informally, the slope of a line in a coordinate plane is the quotient of the change in the vertical direction divided by the change in the horizontal direction that is necessary to get from one point to another.

I consider myself to be a fluent reader. I read comfortably and with meaning in a wide range of texts including fiction, nonfiction, and poetry. Yet, in that passage on coordinate geometry, I cannot make meaning. I can read with fluency. I can say all of the words. To an observer listening to me read orally, I might sound pretty good. But, I have no clue what the passage means. Having devoted my twenty-nine-year career in education to literacy instruction, I have very little background in math. A caring support person could have made that passage easier by helping me build understanding with manipulatives and a demonstration before I attempted to read . . . but on my own, I am lost.

It is critical that readers understand the importance of their prior knowledge. They must learn that reading passages on familiar topics will be easier than reading about new ideas and experiences. They must also develop a range of strategies for consciously and thoughtfully activating their prior knowledge before and during reading, then making connections and pulling it all together after reading (Keene and Zimmerman, 1997).

Think alouds provide a framework for laying open the thinking that normally goes on inside the head of a proficient reader. When a teacher or other proficient reader thinks aloud while interacting with a text, the learner has an opportunity to observe how prior knowledge is activated and how the reader moves back and forth between the text and his or her own experiences to create understanding. When engaging in a think aloud, it is very important to make it clear to the students when you are reading from the text and when you are making connections to your experiences. I like to point to the text as I read and then point to myself when I am thinking aloud as a visual support to the message.

> **SNOW**
> Falling
> Drifting
> Sparkling
> Covering the ground like a white blanket
> Burning
> Stinging
> Biting into your flesh
> An icy storm raging across the mountain

The following is an example of how a think aloud on the poem, "Snow," might sound:

THE POEM	THINK ALOUD EXAMPLE
Snow	The Title: SNOW I love snow. I love it when it is first starting to fall and when the ground begins to turn white.
Falling	Falling: That makes me think of the way it seems to come so slowly out of the sky.
Drifting	Drifting: Snow drifts are the best. When the snow is piled up, you can dive into it and slide down the big hills.
Sparkling	Sparkling: I think of the times when the sun has been shining on the snow and it looks like it is full of tiny mirrors and crystals.
Covering the ground like a white blanket	A big thick blanket . . . and it makes everything so quiet!
Burning	Burning: It feels like the poem has changed. The snow isn't soft and beautiful anymore. It is dangerous. This reminds me of skiing when the wind is blowing and the snow isn't soft at all it is hard and stinging ice crystals that feel like needles biting into my face.
Stinging	Stinging and Biting: This is just like it was for me
Biting into your flesh An icy storm raging across the mountain	This makes me think of people hunched over, fighting through snow drifts and pushing against the wind.

Key Questions for Students

- How do we use our prior knowledge when reading?
- What can readers do to help themselves?
- What might we add to our personal or class strategy lists about prior knowledge?

Key Question for Teachers

- What can we as teachers do to provide better schema-building opportunities before reading for children with limited prior knowledge on a topic?
- What can we do to ensure that readers take time to utilize existing prior knowledge as they read?

The following passages are designed to be overhead transparencies to spark conversations about prior knowledge. First, demonstrate a think aloud or two, then guide your students in thinking aloud with the shared passages: What are the clues? What do I know about the world that will help me? Can I confirm what I think? Can I get a picture in my head? Did I have an experience that relates to this? What was my experience like? What connections can I make between my experience and this text? Can I make any connections between this text and another text? Can I make any connections between this text and something I know to be true about the world?

Following your demonstration and guided practice, students could continue their prior knowledge applications in guided reading, literature study, and independent reading. Strategy conversations eventually should return to the class strategy log and/or the students' personal strategy logs.

SNOW

Falling
Drifting
Sparkling
Covering the ground like a white
    blanket

Burning
Stinging
Biting into your flesh
An icy storm raging across the
    mountain

© 2000 by Linda Hoyt from *Snapshots*. Portsmouth, NH: Heinemann.

IN MY BACKYARD

Bounding away with heads held high
Darting back into the trees
Tiny hoof prints left behind
What scared these creatures with
    antlers like trees?

© 2000 by Linda Hoyt from *Snapshots*. Portsmouth, NH: Heinemann.

The School Bus

Chattering kids
Stops and starts
"Sit down and be quiet!"

Big step up
A noisy greeting
Straining up a hill

Bright and yellow
Flashing lights
Stop sign sticking out

Laughing children
Loud and clear
A music of its own

© 2000 by Linda Hoyt from *Snapshots*. Portsmouth, NH: Heinemann.

Newspaper Article

THE OREGONIAN ◆ TUESDAY, DECEMBER 28, 1999

Living Pets
SMART

TAKE ME HOME

SASSY

Intelligent, playful dog would be good with children

Sassy was a stray dog. Thought to be a sheltie/shepherd mix, she is approximately 5 months old and has a soft fur coat. Sassy is smart, playful and sweet. A family with children to play with would be ideal for her.

To learn more about adopting this dog or other animals from Columbia County Animal Control, contact the shelter at 2084 Oregon St., St. Helens. Adoption hours are 11 a.m. to 5 p.m. weekdays; 503-397-3935.

FIGURE 2.2 Reprinted with permission from *The Oregonian*, Portland, Oregon.

Strategy Reflections

What did you already know that helped you understand these passages? In each one, talk about the connections you made to your own experiences and/or readings.

© 2000 by Linda Hoyt from *Snapshots*. Portsmouth, NH: Heinemann.

Visualizing During Reading

A *Peanuts* cartoon once read: *I like reading. It turns on pictures in your head!*

I have always enjoyed that cartoon for I believe that readers who visualize while reading are more likely to construct meaning while they read. Readers who visualize are generating images that are composites of information gained from the text and their personal knowledge of the world. These are the very connections that research indicates signal comprehension (Pearson, 1999) and lead to strategic interactions with text.

To help students understand how to visualize, I start with familiar shared events. For example:

> *Remember yesterday when we were taking a walk with our writers notebooks and it started to rain? I remember the first thing I did was to stuff my notebook inside my jacket so it didn't get wet. I remember the first drops of rain hitting my forehead and running down my nose, then the skies really opened up and I realized that I had to run or be drenched.*
>
> *If you close your eyes and think about that moment, what do you see? What do you feel? What did you look like? Can you describe the picture in your head?*

A next step might be to read a really descriptive passage from a text and ask the students to try to imagine the scene as if it were a movie playing in their heads (Dionisio, 1998). This requires more dependence on imagination than a real experience so it is critical to provide plenty of time for the visualization as well as for conversation during and after reading. A think aloud with a passage or two may help students have a deeper understanding of the process of translating a passage into visual images and the way that you might need to stop occasionally to synthesize information and add it to your visual image, or to make personal connections. (See page 44.)

As a follow-up, students enjoy playing a version of Pictionary focused on their guided reading or literature-circle selections. One student draws to represent his or her personal visualization from the story while the others guess what is in the scene and why the illustrator is drawing it.

Key Questions

- As you created your mental picture, were you able to keep adding details as more information was provided?
- Were you able to think about your knowledge and previous experiences to help you understand this better?
- What could you do to help yourself remember to visualize and make movies in your head while you read?

Visualization

Small fish swam everywhere, some narrow and long, some round, most of them three or four inches long, some a bit larger and many smaller.

While he stood some of the small, roundish fish came quite close to his legs and he tensed, got ready and made a wild stab at grabbing one of them. They exploded away in a hundred flicks of quick light, so fast that he had no hope of catching them that way. But they soon came back, seemed to be curious about him, and as he walked from the water he tried to think of a way to use that curiosity to catch them.

He had no hooks or string but if he could somehow lure them into the shallows— and make a small fish spear—he might be able to strike fast enough to get one.

Used with permission from *Hatchet*, page 107, by Gary Paulsen.

© 2000 by Linda Hoyt from *Snapshots*. Portsmouth, NH: Heinemann.

Visualization

It was Saturday. Bingo heard the familiar sounds of cartoons. In his eagerness to be in front of the TV, he almost threw his feet over the side of the bed and jumped off.

He opened his eyes and was instantly grateful he had not leapt. If he had, he would have fallen six feet to Billy Wentworth's floor and broken both his legs.

He spent a few moments looking at Billy Wentworth's ceiling. This was the closest he had ever been to a ceiling. Then he leaned over the side of the bunk. The bottom bunk was empty.

Used with permission from *The Burning Questions of Bingo Brown*, page 112, by Betsy Byars.

© 2000 by Linda Hoyt from *Snapshots*. Portsmouth, NH: Heinemann.

Visualization

From page 4:
Like its prehistoric ancestors, the shark's mouth is still underneath its head. To eat, the shark has to bend its snout and bring its jaws forward so the mouth is out in front and the teeth are bared. Powerful hunters like the great white [shark] may have 20 rows of teeth.

From page 6:
A shark's mouth is not just for eating. Sharks breathe through their mouths. They get oxygen by swimming forward and forcing water into their mouths, past their gills, and out their gill slits. A shark must keep its mouth open when it swims, or it will die.

Used with permission from *Amazing Sharks*, by Melvin Berger, Newbridge Communications, 1996.

© 2000 by Linda Hoyt from *Snapshots*. Portsmouth, NH: Heinemann.

Strategy Challenge

I find that some students can talk about a variety of strategies but show less application in their reading than their descriptions of strategy use would suggest. As a result, I like to engage the students in self-reflections such as the following.

Strategy Challenge

• How do you know when you understand or comprehend?

• Make a list of clues that make it clear you are "getting it!"

(Suggestions: It makes sense . . . I understand . . . I can summarize it . . . I can pick out the important ideas . . . I get a picture in my head.)

• Give at least two specific examples of times you USED a strategy. Be specific about the book, the part of the book, and the strategy you used.

• Give an example of a time when you understood and you KNEW you understood a passage. What were the clues? How did you know you "got it?"

© 2000 by Linda Hoyt from *Snapshots*. Portsmouth, NH: Heinemann.

Personal Reading Assessment

Date _____

Dear _____,

I am learning ways to be a good reader. One important thing I have learned is _____ _____.

A new reading strategy I have learned is _____.

My favorite book is _____.

It was about _____

_____.

I liked it because _____.

While I was reading this book, I used a reading strategy. The strategy was _____

_____.

Sincerely,

© 2000 by Linda Hoyt from *Snapshots*. Portsmouth, NH: Heinemann.

My Personal Strategy Review

Name _____   Date _____

Before reading, I

____ look at the title and pictures

____ think about the topic and what I already know

____ predict

During reading, I

____ confirm or adjust my predictions

____ get a picture in my head

____ make connections to what I already know

____ use fix-up strategies on tricky words

    ____ read on

    ____ backtrack

    ____ look at pictures

    ____ use word parts

    ____ put in another word that makes sense

After reading, I

____ pull it all together in my head and think about the important parts

© 2000 by Linda Hoyt from *Snapshots*. Portsmouth, NH: Heinemann.

It is essential to step back and observe our learners walking their talk—to really assess what is happening when they read and how our minilessons, think alouds, conference feedback, and so on can provide support to observable behaviors. Many students are using effective reader strategies but are doing so unconsciously. Is there a way to acknowledge this use and ensure that the usage will continue? Other students need more explicit support to transfer strategy use from minilessons to independent use. How might they get the scaffolding they need? Are there some students who caught onto part of a strategy but are using it incorrectly and need to clarify the purpose and use of the strategy?

The following assessment tools are possibilities to consider, but all continue to emphasize diverse and flexible reading strategies.

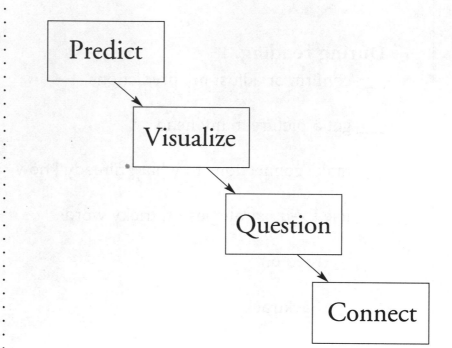

Reading Log

Reader _____

			Strategies Used										Retell						
	Key: + Strategy effectively used • Strategy taught in conference		Picture clues	Prediction	Read on	Re-read	Sound it out	Self-correction	Makes connections	Substitutes meaningful words	Reading rate appropriate to text		Characters	Setting	Problem/Solution	Theme	Events	Nonfiction/key ideas	Nonfiction connections
Date	Book	Page(s)																	

© 2000 by Linda Hoyt from *Snapshots*. Portsmouth, NH: Heinemann.

Strategy Scoring Guide

A self-monitoring reader understands that a variety of strategies are available and a good reader selects strategies as needed to match the demands of the text.

6 The advanced strategy user employs the full range of self-monitoring strategies and easily shifts strategies in response to the demands of varying texts. This reader thoughtfully and purposefully uses:

√ picture clues

√ graphic supports such as charts and boldfaced type

√ shifts in reading speed to respond to the text

√ self-questioning before and during reading

√ making connections to prior knowledge

√ re-reading

√ reading on for more context

√ analysis of word parts

√ synthesizing of information

4 The developing strategy user employs some self-monitoring strategies and is still learning to shift strategies to match the demands of different texts. This reader may use strategies effectively with texts in his or her comfort zone, but abandon a broad base of strategies and return to "sounding out" in texts that may feel too difficult.

√ picture clues

√ graphic supports such as charts and boldfaced type

√ shifts in reading speed to respond to the text

√ self-questioning before and during reading

√ making connections to prior knowledge

√ re-reading

√ reading on for more context

√ analysis of word parts

√ synthesizing of information

Continues

© 2000 by Linda Hoyt from *Snapshots*. Portsmouth, NH: Heinemann.

Strategy Scoring Guide *continued*

2   The emerging strategy user utilizes one or two strategies and lacks both an understanding of the full range of strategies and the way strategies are shifted in response to changing texts. This reader relies heavily on coaches and other readers for reminders to use diverse strategies.

√ picture clues

√ graphic supports such as charts and boldfaced type

√ shifts in reading speed to respond to the text

√ self-questioning before and during reading

√ making connections to prior knowledge

√ re-reading

√ reading on for more context

√ analysis of word parts

√ synthesizing of information

© 2000 by Linda Hoyt from *Snapshots*. Portsmouth, NH: Heinemann.

Reading Profile

Student _____

Text _____ Date _____

Cueing System Percentages

Percentage	Meaning	Structure	Visual	Self-correct
100				
90				
80				
70				
60				
50				
40				
30				
20				
10				

Substitution Comparison

Miscues	Child	Text	Meaning	Structure	Visual	Self-correct
1						
2						
3						
4						
5						
6						
7						
8						
9						
10						
Total						

Implications for Instruction

_____

_____

_____

_____

_____

Counts of Strategy Use
(Tally or comment)

Meaning (Semantic Cues)
"Does it make sense?"
   Reads on _____
   Backtracks _____
   Self-corrects _____
   Meaningful substitutions_____
   Picture clues _____

Structure (Syntactic Cues)
"Does it sound right?"
   Uses grammar _____
   Word order_____
   Noun/verb agreement _____

Visual (Grapho-Phonic Cues)
"Does it look right?"
   Uses beginning sounds _____
   Ending sounds _____
   Chunks words _____

Adapted from the work of Goodman *et al.* and Clay.

© 2000 by Linda Hoyt from *Snapshots*. Portsmouth, NH: Heinemann.

Running Record Form

Name _____   Date _____

Reading Level
___Independent
___Instructional
___Challenging

Name of Book: _____   Level of Book: _____

| Words ___ ___ | Error Rate___% | Accuracy Rate___% (A–Z) or (1–44) | Self-Correction Rate___% |
| Errors | | | |

E	SC	Text	Errors			Self-Corrections			Comments
			M	S	V	M	S	V	

Adapted from the work of Marie Clay.

Emergent Literacy Profile

This three-part assessment is designed to assess a wide range of literacy development over time. Based on the needs of the child, it may be appropriate to use in its entirety or only to use the parts that are necessary to inform instruction. If it is used as a pre- and post-assessment, you may wish to use two colors of ink. Scoring is optional, depending on your purpose.

Student: _____   Recorder: _____

Date: _____ Title: _____   Level of text: _____

Date: _____ Title: _____   Level of text: _____

1. **Strategies: (Teacher reads: 1 point each,**
   Child reads: 2 points each)
   _/_ Knows where the story starts   Notes:
   _/_ Moves left to right/top to bottom
   _/_ Uses illustrations for cues
   _/_ Matches voice to print
   _/_ Uses sense of story (meaning) for cues
   _/_ Uses sense of language (structure) for cues
   _/_ Uses consonant sounds (visual) for cues
   _/_ Self-corrects when reading does not make sense
   _/_ Reads on past unknown words/backtracks
   _/_ Makes meaningful substitutions

2. **Understanding the Story: (Listening or Reading)**   Total ___/___

Makes meaningful predictions	0	1	2	3	4	5

Retells the story in own words

characters	0	1	2	3	4	5
setting	0	1	2	3	4	5
events	0	1	2	3	4	5
main idea (problem/solution)	0	1	2	3	4	5
Has an opinion about the story	0	1	2	3	4	5

If you read to the child: **Total** ___/___

If child reads, multiply the total by 2 **Total** ___/___

Continues

© 2000 by Linda Hoyt from *Snapshots*. Portsmouth, NH: Heinemann.

Emergent Literacy Profile *continued*

3. Stages of Reading and Writing: (Use multiple reading and writing samples to determine a child's stage. If you wish to score, circle the corresponding number and record the total for this section.)

	Roleplay	Experimental	Early	Transitional	
Stage of Reading	2	4	6	8	10

	Roleplay	Experimental	Early	Conventional	
Stage of Writing	2	4	6	8	10

Total ____/____

Implications for Instruction:

Overall Total ____/____

100 points possible

© 2000 by Linda Hoyt from *Snapshots*. Portsmouth, NH: Heinemann.

3

Showtime!
A Celebration of Oral Reading

I believe that oral reading serves two purposes: (1) to offer a window into what a reader is doing during an interaction with text, and (2) to celebrate wonderful language.

The Way to Assess

With that in mind, I believe that assessment should happen in a private moment between a child and a literacy coach. If I am listening to a child with the purpose of developing an understanding of what that child does or does not know about print, I make sure the child and I are in a relatively private space so that I am not measuring reading proficiency plus stress. Round robin reading, where one child reads and others listen (Opitz and Rasinski, 1999), should never be used for assessment purposes as there are too many variables and too much social pressure for a child to be at his or her best.

Rehearsals

Celebration of wonderful language requires rehearsal. When you share something special, you want to practice reading it so that it is read with the drama, inflection, and pace appropriate to the meaning and style. As a result, I tell students that they need to rehearse if they want to read orally to celebrate. This has multiple benefits because repeated readings naturally enhance fluency and pace.

The following Snapshots are invitations to create situations where multiple readings of a text are fun and enjoyable, never tedious.

Reading with Meaning

Children, do your homework.

Make a transparency of this page. When you place it on the overhead, place a piece of paper on the line above so that all children can see is the line that says: Children, do your homework. For your demonstration, read this as though you were really grumpy, then really old and weak . . . Read it like you are a sweet grandma trying to show love. . . . Talk about the differences. The words are the same but the meaning changed. Invite the students to read it with you using different styles and intonations. Try it again with these additional examples:

It's time for bed.

Don't forget to feed the dog.

Your dentist appointment is today.

Send students on a search for sentences in their books that they can read with a variety of inflections and then invite them to share with each other.

© 2000 by Linda Hoyt from *Snapshots*. Portsmouth, NH: Heinemann.

Performing Our Favorite Stories

For this minilesson, I make an audio- or videotape of myself reading a fairly brief picture book then ask the students to listen to my tape while I turn the pages of the book. I explain that my goal is to perform the book for the Head Start students when they come to visit, so I want to be sure my reading is as interesting as possible. Their job is to offer compliments and suggestions for my reading. I use a T-chart such as the one below to record their observations.

COMPLIMENTS	SUGGESTIONS

Then, I read the book to the students, being as dramatic as possible and trying to implement their suggestions. Again, I ask them for compliments and suggestions.

For Guided Practice

I have students work in teams of two to select books, talk about reading dramatically, and rehearse. When they feel they are ready, they can present the book to another partner pair and ask for compliments and suggestions.

For Independent Practice

Each child selects a book, rehearses until ready, then performs for a friend following the compliments-and-suggestions format. I encourage them to make a tape recording of their reading, listen to it, and follow the compliments-and-suggestions format on themselves.

Lastly, we often make audiotapes of our read alouds and give them to the parents or local Head Start as a gift, or offer to be guest readers for students in other classrooms.

Key Questions

- What are the attributes of a good oral reading?
- What do I notice about my reading when I practice?
- How can my partners help me improve my oral reading?

Performing Readers Theater Straight from the Book

Using a transparency of a text, photocopies of a text, or individual student copies of a book, I start this minilesson by explaining how writers use quotation marks to show when someone is speaking and how it is a reader's job to identify the speaker and change the voice to sound like the character. Readers also have the job of adjusting the speed of their reading to match the meaning of the text. For example, serious texts need to be read more slowly than silly poetry.

If I am working with photocopies, I give the students highlighter pens and ask them to highlight the parts that fall within quotation marks so they can clearly see the dialogue. I can achieve the same goal with purchased highlighter tape that allows the text to show through and is removeable.

Once this is done I read aloud for a bit, making exaggerated use of voice changes for characters and narrator. After the demonstration, I explain to the students that they will be reading the dialogue and I will read the narrator's part, so they begin to get a sense of the voice changes. After a brief amount of reading, I suggest that we stop, return to the beginning, and trade parts. I then do the dialogue and the students as a group read the narrator's part. This has several benefits. First, when students read in unison, they often read a bit faster than if they were on their own. The group carries individuals over the hard parts and maintains a flow of language and rhythm that isn't always in place when one child reads aloud an unrehearsed text. We are also benefiting from re-reading the text. The students are reading it again, but also vocalizing a different part so it still feels meaningful and authentic.

As the students appear to be ready, I take them through the following opportunities:

1. Divide the group in half. One team reads dialogue, the other narrative. Then trade.
2. Assign character parts. A caution here: sometimes characters don't speak very often and a student has to wait too long for a turn. When that is the case, I have them represent several characters. For example: "Johnny and Allen, please be all of the Billy Goats for this reading." In other cases, the text doesn't explicitly name the speaker, so you have to determine who it is by looking at the speaking turns being taken.

Finally, we review the text for ways to add drama to our reading and then plan a performance.

If you use the following *Three Billy Goats Gruff* samples or poetry, before proceeding please make sure the students know the story, have activated prior knowledge, or have experienced the text as a read aloud.

Key Questions

- How can we add smoothness to our oral reading?
- How can we change the tone and volume of our voices to add interest for a listener?
- What speed of reading will match this selection?

Readers Theater: The Three Billy Goats Gruff

Once upon a time, there were three billy goats. The biggest billy goat was hungry and he said, "I am really hungry! Let's go to that green hillside and eat some of that good green grass."

The middle billy goat was hungry too and he said, "Let's go!"

The smallest billy goat cried, "Me too!"

On the way to the hill, they had to cross the bridge where the big, old troll lived.

Big Billy Goat said, "Hey, Little Billy Goat, why don't you go across first and I will watch out for the troll."

Little Billy Goat started walking across the bridge. Trip, trap, trip, trap went the bridge.

The Troll jumped up and said, "You can't walk on my bridge! I am going to eat you up!"

Little Billy Goat said, "You don't want to eat me. My big brother is coming soon and he is much bigger than me."

Continues

   © 2000 by Linda Hoyt from *Snapshots*. Portsmouth, NH: Heinemann.

Readers Theater *continued*

So the Little Billy Goat jumped off the bridge and watched to see what his big brother would do.

The middle brother had been watching and had an idea.

"Hey, Big Brother. Why don't you go across the bridge and I will sneak up on the Troll from the other side."

"Good thinking, Middle Brother. That will really surprise that nasty old Troll."

So the Big Billy Goat started walking across the bridge. TRIP, TRAP, TRIP, TRAP went the bridge.

The Troll jumped up and said, "You can't walk on my bridge! I am going to eat you up!"

Just then the Middle Brother came running from behind the troll and bumped him right off the bridge.

The Troll wasn't hurt but he was so surprised that he never bothered the three billy goats again.

© 2000 by Linda Hoyt from *Snapshots*. Portsmouth, NH: Heinemann.

Readers Theater: Poetry

Eagle

Soaring
Gliding
Searching for a meal

Plunging
Spiraling
Diving toward its prey

Majestic
Regal
Symbol of our nation
Fighting for survival

© 2000 by Linda Hoyt from *Snapshots*. Portsmouth, NH: Heinemann.

PUMPKINS

Orange
Yellow
Some are round
Some are fat
Some are thin
Some to keep your candy in

© 2000 by Linda Hoyt from *Snapshots*. Portsmouth, NH: Heinemann.

Poetry can be ideal for demonstrating a wide range of reading rates. Some poems call for fast and lively reading, while others are slow and dramatic and need many pauses for emphasis. In either case, readers theater offers opportunities to explore the piece with multiple voices. Students could take turns reading every other line. They might try reading with a finger snap, a hand clap, or dramatic actions. The rules are few. I demonstrate with a number of poems and then turn them loose to read poetry books and discover how multiple voices and rehearsal can turn a poem into a celebration of fluent reading.

Key Questions
- Which poems are best at which rates?
- How does rate or pace affect meaning for the listener?

Readers Theater: Expository Text

Children enjoy writing their own readers theater scripts by rewriting favorite stories, going through novels to select key dialogue and narrative, or turning science and social studies writings into scripts that they can read aloud and perform with the assistance of some friends.

Abraham Lincoln

Narrator 1: In 1809, Abraham Lincoln was born in a log cabin in Kentucky. He moved a lot as a child.

Narrator 2: When he was nine, his mother died, leaving his father to take care of Abe, his sister, and his second cousin.

Narrator 3: A year later, Abe's father left on a trip and the kids were left at home for many weeks.

All: When his father returned, he had a new wife.

Narrator 3: Abraham studied hard to learn to read and write. He was also a hard worker. He cut wood and even worked on the Mississippi River.

Narrator 1: As a young man, he was nicknamed Honest Abe.

Narrator 2: In 1832, he ran for the legislature . . .

All: but he lost.

Narrator 3: In 1834, he ran again . . .

Narrator 2: but placed second.

Narrator 1: On his third try, he won.

All: Lincoln became a lawyer . . .

Narrator 1: after many years of teaching himself about the law.

Narrator 2: He married Mary Ann Todd.

Narrator 3: In 1846, he became a Congressman and moved to Washington, D.C.

All: Lincoln became a leader in antislavery efforts.

Narrator 1: He was elected president and tried to hold the union together.

Narrator 3: Two years after declaring that all black people were free . . .

Narrator 2: and one year after the end of the Civil War . . .

All: Abraham Lincoln was shot to death . . . but his memory will always be with us.

© 2000 by Linda Hoyt from *Snapshots*. Portsmouth, NH: Heinemann.

Rhythm and Music to Support Oral Reading

I have discovered that children take particular joy in enhancing their oral reading with rhythm and music. I have several small electronic keyboards that are equipped with a variety of rhythms. The children like to play the various rhythms and experiment with poetry and predictable books. They read their selections over and over as they test the rhythms to see which ones match their reading selections.

This entices them to engage in repeated readings in a fun and authentic format as they are genuinely seeking an answer to a question: Which rhythm fits the text the best?

FIGURE 3.1 Students experimenting with rhythms while reading.

I also find that soft background music can make a tremendous difference in the dramatic affect of a read aloud. I got this idea by listening to a Gary Paulson book on tape of *Dog Song*. During the first ten minutes of the tape, music was playing. When the music stopped, I noticed it immediately and I realized how much less dramatic the reading sounded. Since then, I have started a collection of easy listening tapes, the kind of music I enjoy listening to for a special dinner. I make these available to students who are preparing a read aloud. Even if the students are only reading a paragraph or two as an example of beautifully descriptive language, the music makes a huge difference in the way the reading affects the listeners and the readers themselves.

Key Questions

- Language has natural rhythm. How can we make that rhythm more apparent to listeners?
- How can music enhance my oral reading and remind me that fluent reading isn't always fast . . . sometimes it is filled with dramatic pauses for emphasis?

Fast and Slow Reading

This minilesson is a focus on pacing and rate, an opportunity to demonstrate how rate does change according to the demands of the text.

You could use a big book, a read aloud, or guided reading books.

I start by asking the students to listen to me read and tell me how it sounds. I read really fast, stop and ask for feedback, and then read very slowly, one word at a time.

I engage the children in a conversation about reading rate. How fast is fast enough? How do you know? Do you read at the same rate all of the time? Which books might be fun to read a bit faster? Which ones might you want to read slowly? Why? Does it sound like reading when you read one word at a time?

Over time, we develop a chart like the following to reflect our thinking:

BOOKS TO READ FAST	BOOKS TO READ SLOWLY
Chicka Chicka Boom Boom	*Knots on a Counting Rope*
The Cat in the Hat	*Chickens Aren't the Only Ones*

For guided practice, I have students work with partners and use "thumbs up and thumbs down" to coach each other on rate. If the listener thinks the reading needs to speed up a bit, he can signal the reader with a thumbs up signal. If the reading needs to slow down, a thumbs down signal comes from the listener. The students then add the book to the appropriate column on the Books to Read Fast and Slow chart.

For independent reading, I open with a reminder about rate and ask the students to self-monitor their silent reading rate. The independent reader's job is to be really aware of their own rate and to try to think in terms of matching their rate to the kind of text. At the end of independent reading, we reflect and debrief.

Key Questions
- Which reading rates match which books?
- How can I self-monitor my rate?

Scoring Guide for Fluency and Expression

5 The reader reads with expression.

The rate matches the style of the text.

The reader adjusts tone and emphasis to reflect meaning.

The reading reflects an understanding of audience.

Pauses are used for emphasis.

Self-corrections and fix-up strategies are employed so smoothly the listener does not notice them.

3 There is some expressiveness in the reading.

There is an attempt to match the rate to the text.

The reader may overexaggerate tone in an attempt to be dramatic.

The reader is concentrating so much on the print, that there is only some connection to the audience.

There are pauses for word recognition rather than to emphasize meaning.

Disruptions may occur as the reader attempts to implement reading strategies.

1 The reader reads word by word in a monotone.

There is no evidence of changes in tone, speed, or inflection to match meaning.

The pace is slow and not reflective of the text.

There are frequent pauses for sound outs, repeats of words, and time to look at pictures to construct meaning.

© 2000 by Linda Hoyt from *Snapshots*. Portsmouth, NH: Heinemann.

4

. . . .

Phonemic Awareness
Using Our Ears to Make Sense of Sounds

Phonemic awareness, the ability to auditorily discriminate sounds in words, has been identified by some researchers as a key predictor of success in reading (Adams, 1990; Stanovich, 1994).

In considering phonemic awareness instruction, it is important to remember that it is a function of the ear and is not related to sound-symbol (visual) cues. When we listen to language, we hear streams of sounds that include words and parts of words, yet it is the meaning that captures our attention. As communicators, we naturally listen to hear *what* the words are telling us. Phonemic awareness is about looking *behind* the meaning and bringing those words and parts of words to a conscious level, about noticing sound segments such as phrases, words, syllables, rhymes, and individual sounds. Phonemic awareness can be a wonderful opportunity to take advantage of the natural human tendency to enjoy the sounds of language, to delight in alliteration, rhythm, rhyme (Pinnell and Fountas, 1998), and the feel of words on our tongues.

Phonemic awareness is nurtured when children engage in language and word play, recite poetry rich in rhymes and alliteration, or stretch words out as they prepare to create text in writing.

It is unfortunate, however, that this purely auditory function that develops naturally in most children as a result of language acquisition, language play, and storybook reading has become the focus of formalized programs and workbook-style activities. These programs attempt to separate phonemic awareness from those rich language contexts that make text meaningful and interesting to children. There is also concern that the workbook-style formats place the emphasis on picture identification rather than on the auditory processing, the actual goal. As an example, phonemic awareness and phonic workbook publishers often use the word *cot* in their worksheets, yet few children today have ever seen a cot or use that word to describe a small portable bed. As a result, the child's attention is placed on picture identification rather than on the auditory components of the word and this example of phonemic awareness is laden with barriers rather than supports.

Goals for Instruction

When planning instruction that is targeted directly to phonemic awareness, I try to keep the following points in mind:

- Phonemic awareness develops naturally when children play with poetry, rhyming, and alliteration. Joyful interaction with rich language is vital (Opitz, 2000).
- Phonemic awareness is not phonics. It is a function of the ear, not the eye.
- Children identify strongly with their names and sincerely enjoy thinking of words that start or end with the same sounds as their own names.
- When working on sound segmenting and blending, make sure the words you choose are not just phonically regular but also represent concepts that are familiar to all of your learners.
- Phonemic awareness will continue to develop through guided reading, shared book experiences, and writing. It is not a prerequisite to or a measure of readiness for literacy learning experiences.

The following phonemic awareness snapshots are examples of playful moments with language and are not meant to be an all-encompassing view of phonemic awareness instruction.

In The Bag!

Take two or three large paper bags and place real objects or full-color photos in each, making sure that each object placed in a bag has a "sound partner" represented in the other bag. Example: If I put a Band-Aid in one bag, I would need to find an object that starts with the letter *b* (book, bagel, box) in the second bag.

Procedure

- Have one student stand in front of each bag. Student #1 reaches into the bag and selects an object to hold but does not lift the object out of the bag. This student then says:

  "I am holding something that starts with _____."
  (The child says the beginning sound of the object, not the letter name.)

- The students standing in front of the other bags reach into their bags to find items that start with the same sound.
- At a signal, each student raises their chosen objects into the air to decide if there is a match in the beginning sounds.

This can be a literacy center activity for teams of students or a whole-class activity where the group has to vote to decide if the objects have matching sounds.

Variations

- Objects that have the same ending sounds.
- Objects that have the same number of syllables.
- Objects that rhyme.

FIGURE 4.1 Students playing In the Bag.

You DON'T Say!

Select poetry with a strong sense of rhyme and rhythm, then practice reading it aloud to ensure that the rhyming words are highly predictable. As you read the selections to your students, stop now and then and encourage the children to guess the rhyming word. Remember, this is just an oral interaction, you don't need a chart or a big book to do this. I have found it helpful to keep a file of terrific rhyming poetry in a handy place so I can weave *You DON'T Say* into the many little transitions of the day such as lining up for lunch, changing shoes for PE, and so on.

Examples

One two, buckle my _____.
Three four, shut the _____.
Five six, pick up _____.

Mary had a little lamb
It's fleece was white as snow
And everywhere that Mary went
The lamb was sure to _____.

Left to the window,
Right to the door,
Up to the ceiling,
Down to the _____.

The autumn leaves come dancing down,
Leaves of crimson, gold and _____.

© 2000 by Linda Hoyt from *Snapshots*. Portsmouth, NH: Heinemann.

Name Games

Children naturally identify with their names and enjoy seeing their own names used during the day.

Just Like Me

VERSION 1:

Have the children walk around the room and try to find something that starts with the same sound as their name, then show the group what they found.

EXAMPLES:

<u>R</u>obin found a <u>r</u>uler.

<u>B</u>en found a <u>b</u>ook.

<u>S</u>asha found a <u>s</u>occer ball.

<u>M</u>egan found <u>M</u>ichael.

VERSION 2:

Show the children how you can clap out the number of "beats" in a word. For example, if you clap while you say "book," you can easily identify one "beat." If you clap the word helicopter, you can identify four "beats."

The children enjoy clapping to hear the syllables in the names of their classmates.

EXAMPLES:

Megan	=	2 claps
Angela	=	3 claps
Miguel	=	2 claps
Ben	=	1 clap

Once they catch on, invite them to count the number of syllables (claps) in their own name, then find a partner whose name uses the same number of claps.

PARTNERS:

Megan (2)/Krissy (2)

Mark (1)/Jack (1)

Jennifer (3)/Angelo (3)

Innovating with Familiar Stories

Oral Play

VERSION 1:

Invite the children to orally play with the language of familiar stories, inserting their own names and a corresponding word that starts with the same sound as their name. This is particularly motivating if you use photographs of the children and the corresponding object.

Brown Bear, Brown Bear, What do you see? (Bill Martin, Jr.) can turn into

> <u>M</u>egan, Megan. What do you see? I see a <u>m</u>oose looking at me.
> <u>C</u>arlo, Carlo. What do you see? I see a <u>c</u>aterpillar looking at me.
> <u>K</u>yle, Kyle. What do you see? I see a <u>k</u>ite looking at me.

FIGURE 4.2 <u>D</u>aniel and his <u>d</u>og.

Making the Most of
Sentence Stems

Sentence stems can create interest in phonemic similarities. Children enjoy using the names of their classmates to complete stems such as:

Sergio can sing.
Jamal can jump.
Billy can ride a bike.

Mark likes to eat mushrooms.
Gracie likes to eat grapes.
Eric Smith likes to eat spaghetti.

Peter punches playfully.
Megan makes marmalade.
Josh jumps in jelly.

Elkonian Boxes

Elkonian boxes can be used to help students become more aware of the number of sounds in a word. I like to make a transparency so the boxes show up easily on the overhead projector and keep a cup filled with pennies or other markers handy.

Demonstrating on the Overhead

The students and I work together to work out the number of sounds in a word. Please remember that the number of sounds in a word is not the same as the number of letters. In *kite*, for example, there are three sounds but four letters.

To use an Elkonian box with the word *kite*, you could stand at the overhead and ask the children to help you think about the sounds in the word. You might prompt them with questions such as:

"*Kite*. How does it start?"

As the students respond with the sound not the letter name, you would place a penny in box 1.

"What do you hear next? K. . . . *I*"

As the students provide the second sound, a penny could be placed in box 2, and so on.

To finish: "Let's count and see how many sounds we heard in *kite* . . ."

VARIATION:

Say a word such as *mop* . . .

Ask the student to put a marker in the box where they hear *p*.

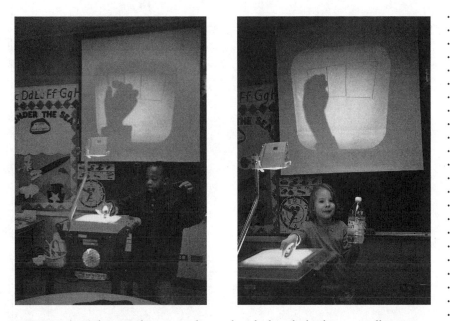

FIGURE 4.3 This minilesson can be used with the whole class, a small group, or as a literacy center.

After demonstrating Elkonian boxes on the overhead and ensuring that students understand how to use the boxes, they can become a meaningful center activity where the students have pictures of objects and place pennies on the boxes for sounds.

Elkonian Boxes Template

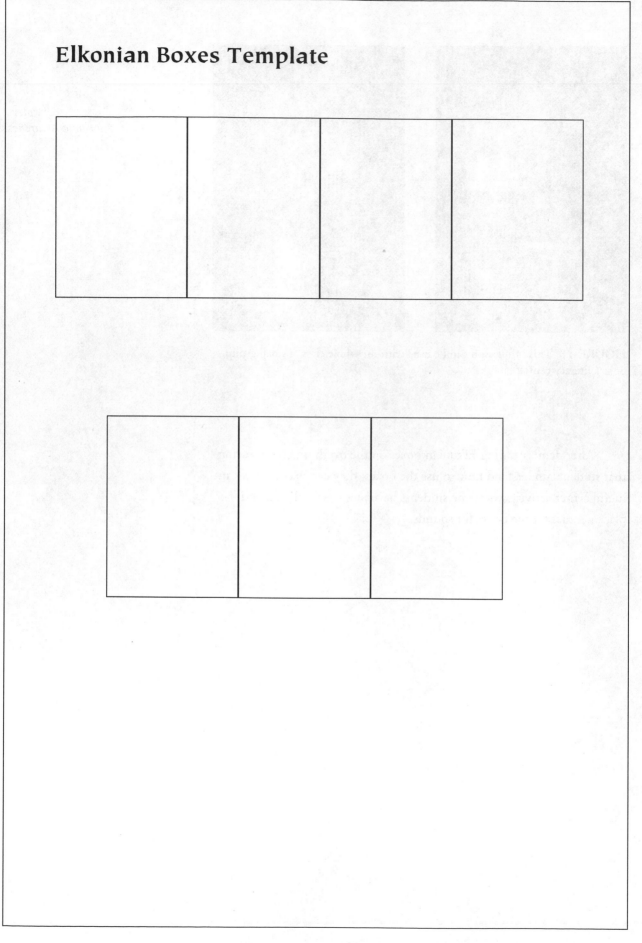

 © 2000 by Linda Hoyt from *Snapshots*. Portsmouth, NH: Heinemann.

Sing It Out

The following songs are templates for playing with sounds and words. As you look at the following examples, please remember to use words that are meaningful and highly familiar to your students. Please also remember the importance of demonstration. It is important to sing the songs for the children and show them explicitly how you stretch a word into isolated sounds or say a word very slowly and then pull it back together. (I find that it is helpful to add visual support to these songs by pulling your hands slowly apart when you want the children to stretch a word.) In the following sample songs, I have used the word *DOG* as it is a highly familiar concept to the children and its sounds can each be clearly distinguished. The goal is to experiment with lots of different words and sing these songs often.

"Row, Row, Row Your Boat"

Clap, clap, clap the sounds

Listen to the parts

Hear the sounds and clap them out

Clap the sounds you hear

DOG   D O G

(Say the word)   (Clap as you say
                          each sound. Do not
                          say the letter name)

© 2000 by Linda Hoyt from *Snapshots*. Portsmouth, NH: Heinemann.

"Row, Row, Row Your Boat"

Stretch, stretch, stretch this word

Pull the sounds apart

Use your ears and listen well

What sounds do you hear?

DOG	D . . . O . . . G
(Say the word)	(Students stretch it out . . . say the sounds slowly)

© 2000 by Linda Hoyt from *Snapshots*. Portsmouth, NH: Heinemann.

"Row, Row, Row Your Boat"

Squeeze, squeeze, squeeze the
     sounds

Pull them all together

Use your ears and listen well

What word do you hear?

D . . .   O . . .   G   DOG

(Stretch it out . . . say   (Students say
the sounds slowly)   the word)

     © 2000 by Linda Hoyt from *Snapshots*. Portsmouth, NH: Heinemann.

"Mary Had a Little Lamb"

Every word has little sounds, little
sounds, little sounds

Every word has little sounds

Turn your ears on now

DOG   D . . . O . . . G

(Say the word)   (Stretch it out)

© 2000 by Linda Hoyt from *Snapshots*. Portsmouth, NH: Heinemann.

"If You Are Happy and You Know It"

If you think you know this word
shout it out (clap, clap)!

If you think you know this word
shout it out (clap, clap)!

If you think you know this word, then
tell me what you've heard

If you think you know this word,
shout it out (clap, clap)

D . . . O . . . G   DOG!

(Say the sounds, not   (Say the word)
the names of the letters)

© 2000 by Linda Hoyt from *Snapshots*. Portsmouth, NH: Heinemann.

5

Building Knowledge of Print
Sounds, Symbols, and Sight Words in Action

Observe → Plan → Teach

Observe: Check for Sound/Symbol Use in Reading and Writing

To ensure that phonics instruction will be meaningful and useful to children, it is critical to understand exactly what a child does or does not know. The International Reading Association (IRA) position paper on reading instruction has made it very clear that we all have a responsibility to identify learner phases of development and areas of need. Then, we teach specifically to those areas (IRA and NAEYC, 1998). The problem with predetermined sequences is that the needs of individual learners are not always taken into consideration. In an era of standards-based teaching and high-stakes benchmarks, every instructional minute counts. As advocates for our children and the torch bearers of accelerated learning, we know that children learn best when their teachers understand their needs and then teach directly to those needs.

When I am planning for phonics instruction, I utilize at least two opportunities for authentic assessment of phonic principles in action. I might first observe the child reading, do a running record, and identify the range of sound–symbol relationships used accurately during reading.

I would then look at unedited writing samples and record on graph paper or a simple chart (see the following Phonic Writing Analysis) the sounds the child used accurately in writing. These two observations will clearly demonstrate which sounds a child has internalized and can apply in real contexts.

In Megan's note about screaming, a quick scan of the page shows that she is using the phoneme *S* appropriately and has used it more than

Phonic Writing Analysis Chart

√ ( ) demonstrations
(√) student understandings

	b	c	d	f	g	h	j	k	l	m	n	p	q	r	s	t
Megan	I		I	I	I					III				II	II	

FIGURE 5.1 Phonic Writing Analysis for Megan.

once. I can place a tally mark on the phonic writing assessment chart under the letter *S* to show the sound/symbol relationship for *S* appears to be emerging, but I would want to confirm this in more than one writing

FIGURE 5.2 Megan writes:

I am

I am sorry

for screaming.

Good bye.

sample before I could confirm her ownership of the phoneme. I would also give Megan a tally on the chart for the letter *M* as it was used in screaming and in the word *AM*. She used the sound/symbol relationships correctly for *g*, *d*, and *b* as well. I can quickly see where I might direct minilessons to support Megan's exploration of additional sounds. As you can see, a pattern begins to build very quickly that provides a window into the sounds and symbols a student, a group of children, or an entire classroom may benefit from exploring.

Instructional materials often mandate an instructional order for sound–symbol relationships. This is very dangerous as it ignores learner knowledge and development and risks having children spend precious time rehearsing sounds they are already using. A phonic writing analysis is systematic, explicit, and responsive to observable learner need.

Once the phonic writing analysis is developed, instruction can be organized in a manner that is highly accountable. Preprogrammed phonics materials that dictate an order for phonics instruction run the risk of wasting learner time by practicing sounds that are already within the learner's repertoire. The Phonic Writing Analysis ensures learners will receive instruction targeted directly to individual needs and allows for careful monitoring of progress over time.

Data is collected throughout the year on the Phonic Writing Analysis and it forms a foundation for integrating assessment and instruction. I check it continually as I am planning minilessons for individuals, for small groups, and for the whole class. I also refer to it as I am supporting children in writing to see if new sounds are being applied in their writing.

Plan: Understand Which Sounds Have the Highest Levels of Utility

The Phonic Writing Analysis that follows and my running records of a child's reading provide very clear overviews of the phonemic elements that are understood and applied by a reader. My next task is to consider what I know about high-utility phonic understandings and to plan my phonic minilessons.

Focus on High-Utility Relationships

Scores of researchers and practioners have engaged in reviews of phonic relationships to determine which are most useful and most consistent in the English language (Pinnell and Fountas, 1998). The following list of phonic understandings represents those relationships that are both high in utility for reading and writing, and have a reasonably high rate of consistency within our language.

- beginning consonants
- ending consonants

- consonant digraphs (*sh*, *th*, *ch*, *wh*)
- medial consonants
- consonant blends
- long vowels
- short vowels

As we observe our learners and plan instruction to help them build a full repertoire of phonic understandings, these principles can be easily and naturally addressed within the daily, authentic contexts of reading and writing.

Teach: Stimulate Long-Term Memory Through Connections to Real Reading and Writing

Utilize techniques that ground the learning in real texts.

The goal is to provide direct instruction in identifying common patterns while engaging the learners with real books, authentic writing tasks, and additional time with text.

This is not accidental learning. It is explicit, intentional teaching following the gradual release of responsibility model. You teach the phonetic understanding, demonstrate its use in an authentic text, support and scaffold practice, then provide an opportunity to use the phonics knowledge independently.

A second copy of the Phonic Writing Analysis chart such as the following helps me to keep a record of my minilessons. I label a fresh copy of the analysis, Demonstrations. Then, every time I do a phonics demonstration, I place a tally in the appropriate box and I can see, over time, if there are principles I have overly addressed or omitted.

Phonic Writing Analysis Chart
(✓)demonstrations
( )student understandings

	ă	ĕ	ĭ	ŏ	ŭ	ā	ē	ī	ō	ū					
Mini Lessons	|||					||	||					

FIGURE 5.3 Phonic Writing Analysis chart used for recording demonstrations.

Phonic Writing Analysis

( ) student analysis
( ) demonstration checklist

NAME	b	c	d	f	g	h	j	k	l	m	n	p	q	r	s	t	v	w	x	y	z	a	e	i	o	u	sh	ch	th	wh	Silent e
2.																															
3.																															
4.																															
5.																															
6.																															
7.																															
8.																															
9.																															
10.																															
11.																															
12.																															
13.																															
14.																															
15.																															
16.																															
17.																															
18.																															
19.																															

© 2000 by Linda Hoyt from *Snapshots*. Portsmouth, NH: Heinemann.

Writing Analysis

( ) student analysis
( ) demonstrations

Name	-ing	-ed	Contractions	Compounds	Prefixes	Suffixes	Periods	Capitals-sentences	Capitals-	proper nouns	Commas-	sequence phrase	Question marks	Quotation marks	Exclamation	Paragraph indent	Effective word choice	Complete sentences	Maintain focus	Beginning-	Middle-	End-	Interesting Leads

Structural Analysis: -ing, -ed, Contractions, Compounds, Prefixes, Suffixes

Conventions of Print: Periods, Capitals-sentences, Capitals-, proper nouns, Commas-, sequence phrase, Question marks, Quotation marks, Exclamation, Paragraph indent

Language-Structure: Effective word choice, Complete sentences, Maintain focus, Beginning-, Middle-, End-, Interesting Leads

© 2000 by Linda Hoyt from *Snapshots*. Portsmouth, NH: Heinemann.

Pattern Searching

In planning this minilesson, I first identify whether I am planning for a guided reading group, shared book experience, or individual conference. If I am planning for guided reading, I select a phonemic principle that is needed by members of the group. If I am planning for a shared book experience, I select a principle that is needed by a majority of the class. For a reading conference, I target an individual need.

In each of these contexts, the Phonic Writing Analysis chart helps me to target a teaching point needed by the learners.

Using an enlarged text (transparency, chart, or big book), I introduce the target pattern by thinking aloud and pointing out several words that have the pattern. I write the words on a chart and invite the students to add additional words they believe use the same pattern. For guided practice, you might have them practice writing some of the words on wipe-off boards or recreate them using magnetic letters.

The Search

Students work individually or in teams to re-read familiar texts and look for more examples of words that fit the target pattern. They record their "research" and share examples of words that follow the rule and words that were exceptions.

What Is the Pattern?	Examples	Exceptions Found	Books Reviewed
magic *e*	cane	done	*Hungry Caterpillar*
	pole		*Velveteen Rabbit*
	tube		*The Jigaree*

The personal and team research is critical to the process. By returning to familiar books, students are re-reading, which we know builds fluency. Students are increasing time with text, which we know helps overall reading development, AND they are reviewing phonic understandings. Best of all, because they are reviewing phonic understandings in a meaningful context, they can identify whether a word fits the "rule" or is an exception. For example, when working on magic *e* pattern words as in the example above, a student might be tempted to apply the rule to *done* and think everything is fine. However, it is the context, the semantic, and syntactic systems that enable a child to know if their application of phonics is successful or not. This integration of systems increases the likelihood that phonics knowledge will be used to empower the reader.

Key Understandings
- Which patterns in words occur most often in books?
- When I sound out a word and apply phonics, I can also check to see if it makes sense.

Personal Phonics Books

I provide Personal Phonics Books so the students can help me keep track of minilessons and our shared explorations of graphophonics. These little books are 8.5 × 11″ paper stapled into informal books, but the children love them.

Children learn to write the topic of the minilesson at the top of a page and then reserve that page for their reflections on that phonic understanding. As I introduce the lesson, they first check to see if they have started a page on that phonetic principle and then start a new page if needed. Page headings such as *ing*, *ed*, short *o*, *m*, *t*, etc. appear at the top of the pages and reflect our shared explorations. The children keep these books handy during independent reading as well as guided reading and continue to enter examples they find in their reading and writing throughout the curriculum.

Other Uses

The Phonic Writing Analysis continues to help me monitor student progress. I observe their writing, update the analysis chart, and decide whether to review or introduce new understandings in the minilessons for the day.

Personal Phonics Books are also great to:

- Record poetry that uses alliteration and rhyming in such ways that the students notice the phonetic structures.
- Take on print walks. As the students walk around the school, their task is to look for words they can read and then see where they might add the word in their personal phonics book.
- Take home to do environmental print searches.
- "Read the room" and record words into their appropriate phonetic categories.
- Carry into the classroom library and enter new words into their appropriate categories.

Key Understandings

- Words contain common patterns.
- Patterns help me in both writing and reading.
- Many patterns have exceptions.
- Phonics and meaning work together.

Supporting Phonic Understandings

As mentioned in previous chapters, cloze activities help students integrate cueing systems and can be especially helpful for developing phonic understandings. I often take a passage and cover key letters, sounds, or word parts to reinforce particular elements of word study. I use sticky notes to cover word parts in big books, on transparencies on the overhead, or right in their guided reading books.

After covering the target phonemic element, I do a think aloud showing how I would first think about the meaning and then identify the word with the covered sound. Then I show how I would say the word very slowly, stretching out the sounds to try to determine which letter is covered. I encourage the students to watch and listen, but ask them not to participate so they can hear the sounds as I stretch them out.

After I demonstrate this with a word or two, I encourage the students to join in for guided practice. As in the think aloud, we first use meaning to identify the word, then stretch out the sounds to consider the target phoneme. As they begin to participate, I encourage them with comments such as: How do you know? What makes you think so? to ensure that they can replicate this process when working independently.

As they appear to be ready, I have them work in pairs and then individually to follow the same procedure with a photocopy of a familiar text. As they begin independent application, I find that it saves time to either retype the text omitting the target phonemes or to use a felt pen to cover the phonemes on a photocopy of the text. In all cases, they return to the original text to check their work. The return to the original text provides, once again, for repeated re-reading, teaches skimming and scanning for the target words, and clearly demonstrates that there is real-life application for the learning.

Key Understandings
- I can predict words and word parts.
- I use meaning and my knowledge of word patterns to help me read and write.

Cloze to Support Phonic Understandings

Initial Consonant Study

> First of all __ame the youngest __illy __oat __ruff
> to __ross the __ridge. Trip, Trap, __rip, __rap.

Final Consonant Study

> Firs__ of all came the younges__ billy goa__
> Gruf__ to cros__ the bridge. Trip, Trap, Tri__,
> Tra__.

Study of Medial Vowels

> First of all c_me the young_st billy goat Gruff to
> cr_ss the br_dge. Tr_p, Trap, Trip, Tr_p.

© 2000 by Linda Hoyt from *Snapshots*. Portsmouth, NH: Heinemann.

Letter Detectives

For Letter Detectives I select a sound from the Phonic Writing Assessment that a student or a group of students need to work on. After demonstrating the use of that sound in both reading and writing, I have teams of students work together to build a chart such as the one following.

Names of group members: _____ , _____ , _____

Searching for words that start with _____

Our search today will include: ( ) big books ( ) guided reading books
( ) independent reading books ( ) the walls of the room ( ) student-authored books

Book title #1	Book title #2	Other sources
_____	_____	_____
My words	My words	My words
_____	_____	_____
_____	_____	_____
_____	_____	_____
_____	_____	_____

© 2000 by Linda Hoyt from *Snapshots*. Portsmouth, NH: Heinemann.

Key Understandings

- The patterns in letters and sounds stay the same even when I change books.
- There can be lots of words that use the same patterns.

Reading Necklaces

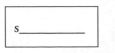

I take a card that has a letter written at the left edge of the card and do a think aloud about the letter. I demonstrate how to find out the sound if I don't know what it is. I can ask a friend. I can go to the word wall and look for words I do know that use the sound. I can look at the alphabet chart and see if the picture helps me.

I write: Mrs. Hoyt likes to *s____*. Each word goes on a separate card. My list of things I like to do might include sing, sit, smile, ski, swing. I explain that I am going to choose the word *ski* because that is something I *especially* like to do.

Mrs. Hoyt likes to ski.

Since each word is on a separate card, I show the students how my sentence can be easily scrambled and put back into meaningful order:

ski Mrs. Hoyt likes to

I also demonstrate reading my sentence to a partner, drawing a picture to go with it, and so on. After I demonstrate multiple ways to read my sentence, I string the sentence onto a piece of yarn and wear it as a necklace so that everyone in the class can practice reading my sentence and asking me questions about what I like to do.

To move into guided practice and independent use, I use the Phonic Writing Analysis on page 95 to identify a sound each child needs to work on, then provide each child with small cards. On one card, the focus sound is written on the left with room to complete the word just as in my demonstration. (I have found it helpful to punch holes in the cards before you distribute them so students can easily weave their yarn through the cards.)

For example, on Anna's Phonic Writing Analysis, I could see that she still was not in control of the letter *W*. So I would write *W* on her card. Anna would then work with a partner to think of things she likes to do that start with *W*. Anna's list might include: wiggle, walk, whisper, work. She makes a decision, creates her sentence, practices scrambling it and reading it with her partner, then strings the sentence on yarn to wear around her neck.

FIGURE 5.4 Reading necklace.

The students have a wonderful time reading each others' necklaces and get a great deal of practice with both phonics and meaningful reading.

Key Understandings

- Words and letters help me to learn about my friends and the world.
- There are lots of words that start with the same letter.
- Letters and words help me to tell about myself.

More Name Games

Children love to see their names in print and are highly motivated when their name appears in multiple locations. The following are just a few ways to engage children in phonics through the use of their names. In all cases, please remember to clearly demonstrate then actively engage the children so they are independently engaged with their learning.

Word Walls

Do a minilesson showing how to put your first name on a sentence strip, then add it to the word wall. Invite the children to work in partners or independently, as is appropriate to their development and add their own names to the wall. (If the children are developmentally ready, be sure to have them alphabetize the words and names under each letter or organize the names and words into separate lists under each letter on the wall. You might even bring in some math by counting the number of names under each letter. Which letters have the most names? How can we tell the names from the words on the word wall?)

Sentence Stems

I like to put a variety of sentence stems onto chart paper and laminate them. I place one stem on each chart and repeat it continuously down the page so many children can participate or one child can explore multiple answers. After the charts are laminated, I run a strip of Velcro down the portion of the chart where the names are listed so the children can quickly sort a collection of class name tags (with Velcro on the back), stick the names onto the chart, and then write the ending of the sentences.

NAMES

    _____Sergio_____   can   _____.

    _____   can   _____.

    _____   can   _____.

    _____   can   _____.

OTHER STEMS TO CONSIDER

    _____ went to _____.

    _____ is really _____.

    _____ is good at _____.

    _____ is from _____.

    _____ likes to read _____.

    _____ hates to _____.

Tongue Twister Stems

Try to write sentences with as many words as possible that start the same as the author's name: Freddy flew to Frank's fort to fry french fries with his friend.

Innovations on Familiar Stories

Create innovations of favorite stories and insert the names of students in the class or ask the students to try to weave in as many words as possible that start with a target sound you have identified from the Phonic Writing Analysis.

Where's Spot? by Eric Hill turns into "Where's Graciella? Is she under the desk? Is she behind the coats?" and so on.

The Bus Ride from Scott Foresman and Celebration Press could turn into "Emily got on the bus. Then the bus went fast. Nahn got on the bus. Then the bus went fast. Celia got on the bus. Then the bus went fast."

The Important Book by Margaret Wise Brown could turn into (target sound *S*) "The Important Thing about Juan is that he likes to swim. He is good at soccer. He likes noodles with sauce. He has two silly sisters. But the important thing about Juan is that he likes to swim."

Traditional tales such as the *Three Billy Goats Gruff* or *The Little Red Hen* could be adjusted by inserting sticky notes into a big book and changing the words. Students have fun changing the names of characters to names of students in class and changing the names of objects in the story into familiar objects in the classroom. Or, using the Phonic Writing Analysis, identify a sound children need to work on and ask them to use sticky notes to change as many story words as they can into words that start with the target sound and still make sense!

Rimes in Action

Did you know that nearly 500 words can be derived from only 37 rimes (Pinnell and Fountas, 1998)? Children love to play with words. As children advance in their understanding of sound–symbol relationships, the following rimes can be placed on cards or charts and used both in minilessons and in guided experiences with rimes.

For a minilesson, I might start by playing with some oral rhyming using the rimes below. I could hold up a card with the letters *ack* and explain that I am going to play with these sounds to see how many words I can come up with that use this combination of sounds. I make a special point to show them how I combine the rime with one- and two-letter onsets.

ack: Back, Black, Crack, Hack, Jack, Mack, Pack, Quack, Rack, Sack, Stack, Tack, Track, Tracker, Zack

Next, for guided practice, I hold up a card with another rime and ask the students to think of all the words they can. As they think of words using that pattern, I write their words on a chart.

In independent practice, children can search for words in their own writing and reading that include these rimes. When an example is found, it could then be placed on a chart for that rime, in a big book of rimes, or in personal phonics books.

(a) ack ail ain ake ale ame an nk ap ask at ate aw ay
(e) eat ell est
(i) ice ick ide ight ill in ine ing ink ip it
(o) ock oke op or ot
(u) uc ut

A Phonics Poetry Game

I start playing with language by selecting a sound and then letting words that start with that sound just roll off my tongue.

EXAMPLE: *D* WORDS

Dog

Dinner

Donuts

Daffodils

Dainty

Dishes

Dirt

Dumb

Dice

I don't try to write . . . just enjoy the sounds of the words. Next, I ask the students to suggest a sound and invite them to join me in a verbal string of words that all start with the sound.

At this point, I can share a poem with alliteration such as the following one.

S is for sailboat

a seal

and a song,

a smile

a seashell

and the sunshine in spring.

(Adapted from *R Is for Ribbon* by Margaret and Travers Moore.)

What letter did the author choose for the focus? If you were going to write a poem like this, what letter would you choose?

Guide the children through the shared writing of a poem using the following transparency template. Read it several times to savor the feel of the words in your mouths.

If the students are developmentally ready to try this independently, you could invite them to work in teams or as individuals to write their own alliteration poetry.

Phonics Fun Poetry!

S is for sailboat

a seal

and a song,

a smile

a seashell

and the sunshine in spring.

_____ is for _____

a _____

and a _____,

a _____

a _____

and the _____ in _____.

© 2000 by Linda Hoyt from *Snapshots*. Portsmouth, NH: Heinemann.

Dot to Dot Scramble

This snapshot works equally well with the overhead projector, a big book, or a guided reading book. This is a good "end of reading" minilesson, as it needs to be used with highly familiar text.

I demonstrate with a think aloud how I might select my favorite sentence from the whole story. Once I have identified a favorite sentence, I show the children how to create a Dot to Dot Scramble.

To make the scramble, I begin by writing the words from my favorite sentence in a mixed up order all around the paper. I place a dot near each word and a big star next to the first word in the sentence just like in the dot to dot books.

Next, I invite two students to see if they can reconnect my words so the sentence is just the way it was in the book. (This may require returning to the original text and re-reading to confirm word order.) The students, with coaching from the rest of the group, connect the words by drawing lines between each word and then check it by reading aloud.

For guided and independent practice, students then create their own dot to dot scrambles with their favorite sentences and have their friends try to read them.

Example: The troll jumped on top of the bridge.

Key Understandings

- Sentences are made up of words.
- Word order is important to meaning.

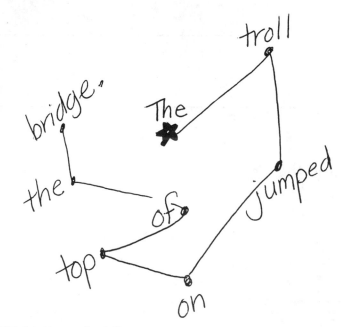

FIGURE 5.5 Dot to dot billy goats game.

FIGURE 5.6 Use yarn to string the sentences back into meaningful order.

Catch the Word!

For this snapshot, I use the overhead to project familiar text onto the screen, then show the students how I can put on my magic gloves (dark gloves) and use a white card (heavy cardstock cut to approximately the height of the words on the screen), to "lift" words right off of the screen.

In my think aloud I might say: "I think I will look for a word with a short *O*" . . . or "I'm looking for a word with an *ing* ending." Then, I place my card in front of the screen so the word I am targeting fits on the card, and then I step forward just a bit. The word is now projected onto my card and is closer to the students than the rest of the text. It is very easy for them to focus on the word as it looks like it has been separated from the rest of the words on the screen. The goal is for the students to examine the word and decide whether it fits the pattern.

For guided practice, students can put on the magic gloves and take turns lifting words with patterns identified by the teacher. They might look for words with a magic *e*, words that start with the letter *b*, or ??? They might also begin to look at quotation marks and lift a section of dialogue from quotation to quotation mark.

FIGURE 5.7 Students hold a card in front of the screen to "catch" words.

To create an opportunity for independent practice, I would put the overhead projector on the floor in a literacy center. The image could shine against the wall and students could work in pairs to take turns lifting words. To help them focus on key phonemic understandings, I provide cards with directions such as: Find a word with the letter *g* at the beginning. Find a word with a short *o*. Find a word with an *ed* ending, and so on.

Add It Up!

To stimulate some word play and integrate a little math, I often ask students to experiment by finding words that are worth a certain monetary value.

For the minilesson, I place the transparency on the following page on the overhead and encourage the students to observe as I try to find a word worth $.50. I might start with my last name to see how much that would be worth on the chart.

$$H = .08$$
$$O = .15$$
$$Y = .25$$
$$T = .20$$

Total = $ .68   Too much!

Now, I can think aloud about my strategies for finding a word that will work a little better. I notice that the letters at the end of the alphabet are worth the most. Will that help me in any way? What strategies might I use to try to find a word worth $.50?

Example: I notice that *Y* is worth $.25. I know that $.25 + .$25 = $.50 . . . So what letters could I add to *Y* that equal $.25? What words start and end with *Y*? I see that *T* is $.20 and *E* is $.05. I can make *YET* and it is exactly $.50!

I notice that students love to bring out books, dictionaries, and their writers notebooks to use as resources. They think hard about consonants, vowels, word length and have a wonderful time doing it.

Variations

- Select three words from the story that all end with the letter *y*. Which one is worth the most?
- Find two words with the magic *e* pattern. Do they follow the rule or are they an exception? How much is each one worth?
- Circle three words that start with the letter *b*. Which one is worth the least?
- Review your writing from today. Find a word with a long vowel. How much is it worth? How many vowels did it have?
- Create wall charts showing words that are worth differing values.

Key Understandings

- Letter order is important in words.
- Not all letters go together.
- It is important to notice the parts of words.

Add It Up!

A	=	$.01	J	=	$.10	S	=	$.19
B	=	$.02	K	=	$.11	T	=	$.20
C	=	$.03	L	=	$.12	U	=	$.21
D	=	$.04	M	=	$.13	V	=	$.22
E	=	$.05	N	=	$.14	W	=	$.23
F	=	$.06	O	=	$.15	X	=	$.24
G	=	$.07	P	=	$.16	Y	=	$.25
H	=	$.08	Q	=	$.17	Z	=	$.26
I	=	$.09	R	=	$.18			

© 2000 by Linda Hoyt from *Snapshots*. Portsmouth, NH: Heinemann.

Three-Letter Word Strategy

To help students learn to alphabetize words, I demonstrate the three-letter word strategy as a quick and fun-filled minilesson.

I start by telling them that I am thinking of a word with just three letters. To find out my word, they need to name words that have three letters but I can only answer: "Your word is before my word in the dictionary" or "Your word is after my word in the dictionary."

Example:

I select the word *hat*.

The first child guesses *mop*. My answer will be: "Your word is after my word in the dictionary."

The second child guesses *bat*. My answer will be: "Your word is before my word in the dictionary."

A third child might say *hug*. (Since this starts with the same letter as my word, I can say: "Your word starts with the same letter as my word AND your word is after my word in the dictionary." This will encourage them to think deeply about words that start with the same sound and have different letters in the second and third position.)

This continues until someone actually guesses my word.

For guided practice, I have the students meet in small groups to play the game. In some cases, it is helpful to have a personal-size copy of the alphabet (see the following example on page 118) in front of them as they play and narrow down their choices. I also find it helpful to have copies of their guided reading books in front of them and encourage the student doing the word selection to pick a word from the story.

Key Understandings

- Words can be alphabetized.
- Letter order is important in words.
- It is helpful to know what letters come in which order in the alphabet.

Three-Letter Word Strategy

The Rules

A "Word Chooser" thinks of a word that has only three letters.

Group members try to figure out the word by naming three-letter words.

The Word Chooser can only answer:

"Your word is BEFORE my word in the dictionary."

"Your word is AFTER my word in the dictionary."

© 2000 by Linda Hoyt from *Snapshots*. Portsmouth, NH: Heinemann.

Personal Alphabet Strips

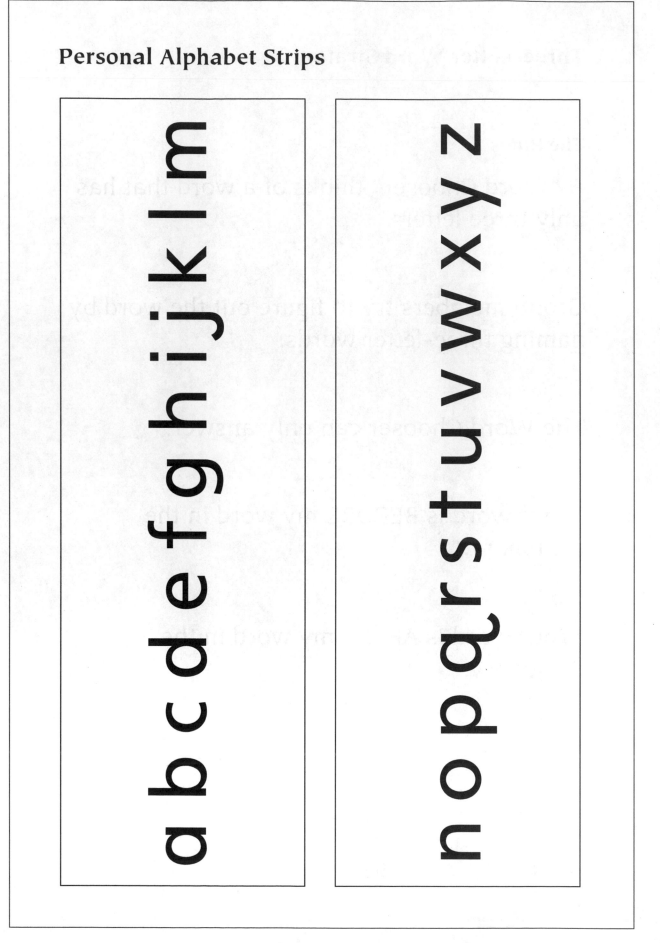

a b c d e f g h i j k l m

n o p q r s t u v w x y z

  © 2000 by Linda Hoyt from *Snapshots*. Portsmouth, NH: Heinemann.

Catalog Catch

I use magazines, newspapers, and catalogs to show children how I can cut out pictures of things I really like. I might cut out a picture of a bicycle, a skateboard, a car, and so on.

Next, using a mural-length section of butcher paper, I write the alphabet across the top edge of the paper, leaving at least 10″ to 12″ between each letter. I am now ready to show the children how I can stretch out the name of each picture and try to decide which letter of the alphabet matches the beginning sound of the picture. For *bicycle*, I would say the word slowly, carefully emphasizing the beginning sound, then go to the chart and glue the picture under the letter *B*.

For guided practice, I encourage students to work in partners and come to agreement about the beginning sound before adding a picture to the chart. I could also refer to the Phonic Writing Analysis and slide cards onto the desks of individuals asking them to search for pictures of things that start with a particular sound.

For independent practice, students could make personal charts or create a pocket book as per the sample shown below.

Variations
- Make a chart for ending sounds, short vowels, long vowels, etc.

Key Understandings
- Words have beginning sounds.
- Sounds and letters go together.

FIGURE 5.8 Catalog catch art.

Little Words in Big Words

I explain to students that when readers are stuck on a word, they sometimes look for little words inside of bigger words. I show them a sentence such as:

The crying child went to the TEACHER for help.

In a think aloud, I model how if I were stuck on the word *teacher*, I would first think of people a crying child might go to for help. It could be a *mom*, a *dad*, a *grandpa*, a *policeman*, a *secretary* at school, a *principal*, a *teacher*, or . . . Now, I can combine making sense with trying to see if there is a little word in the big word that will help me.

I write the letters of the word *TEACHER* on separate cards and place them in a pocket chart or on strips of transparency material on the overhead. Now, I show the children how I can look at the word to see if there are any little words I already know. (Note: I am not trying to scramble letters here, I'm just looking for known chunks in the big word.) Moving the letters around, I separate the following words one at a time, showing the students how they are each a part of the bigger word.

her

each

teach

tea

I then might demonstrate by asking myself the question: Who could a crying child go to that has this little word inside? Could it be policeman? Could it be principal? and so on.

Next, I might read *There's An Ant in Anthony* by Bernard Most and keep a list of all the words that had *ANT* in them in the story.

Finally, I send the children to start reading the room, their independent reading books, and their familiar guided reading favorites to look for little words in bigger words and to share with their partners.

Lastly, I monitor the application of this strategy during writing when the children are crafting spellings and during their independent reading in guided reading and reading conferences to see if the strategy is being implemented in real texts.

Sight Words

The words we encounter most often in reading are often referred to as "sight words," words children need to recognize rapidly in many contexts. If these words are the most commonly occurring, I believe they will be evident in ALL books that are built upon natural language patterns.

As a result, I choose not to have children practice reading sight words on flashcards. My experience has been that children can sometimes get confused and begin to define reading as "naming words" or that they may be able to say the words on the cards, but cannot seem to connect the words within the context of a real book. I also worry that they have no cross-checking mechanism when they are reading words in isolation. Without a meaningful context, there is no way to know if you have misread *was* and *saw* or *where* and *were*. The act of reading demands that we make meaning while we read, thus it is only logical to work on commonly occurring words within a context that allows us to determine if we are or are not making sense.

When children practice sight words in the context of reading and writing real texts, they get the double benefit of increasing their time with text while practicing these words. Also, problems with words that look alike (*when*, *where*, etc.) dissolve if children are focusing on the meaning of what they read. A child who is reading for meaning and cross checking by asking, Is this making sense? would never mistake *was* and *saw* in a sentence like: The girl _____ a candy bar.

As a result, I provide opportunities for students to be reflective about these commonly occurring words and allow plenty of time for them to practice using these words in reading as well as writing. I also provide support to these common words by placing them on the word wall, in personal dictionaries, and by encouraging children to tune in to these words during reading.

Finding Common Words

In this minilesson, I try to help children realize that some words are encountered frequently during reading.

To do this, I place a transparency of a text on the overhead and tell the students that I am going to try to act like a researcher: to read and see which words appear more than once and then ask WHY that word was used so often.

Sample Chart

Word	Tally	WHY? (Related to theme? Common word in language? Could I expect to see this in most every book? Why?)
elephant	√√√	The passage was about elephants
but	√√	Connecting word . . . used in all texts
the	√√√√√√√	It is everywhere!

I read part of the text orally, stopping now and then to tell the students what I notice. For example, "I realize that I have read *and* three times. It was here, and here, and here. I am going to add that to my list of common words," and so on. I need to ask: "Is *and* used because of this story in particular? Is it a word I am likely to see in other books?"

Then, I invite the students to join me in a shared reading of the next section. Their goal is to read for meaning but also to notice which words seem to appear more than once and help me consider them as additions to the chart.

For guided and independent practice, the students and I determine which words from our list are really those we will encounter in many books. Then, we initiate personal and team research projects.

Have children make a grid similar to the one shown below and search favorite books for commonly occurring sight words. This heightens awareness of these common words while providing a great math lesson as well. This can be done over and over again with different words and different books, giving authentic reasons to spend more time reading and more time bringing the most common words into a realm of automatic recognition.

	Mrs. Wishy-Washy	*The Hungry Caterpillar*	*My Bike*
and			
but			
on			
when			

Finding Common Words

	REPEATED WORDS	OTHER BOOKS?
Once upon a time there were three billy goats who lived on a mountainside.	a	yes
There was a very small billy goat named Little Billy Goat Gruff. There was a middle sized billy goat named Middle Billy Goat Gruff. There was a great big billy goat everyone called Big Billy Goat Gruff.	billy goat there, a, was, named	no yes maybe
One day, the three billy goats were hungry so they decided to go up the hill and eat some green grass. To get to the hill, they had to cross a bridge that crossed over a river.		
Little Billy Goat Gruff was really hungry so he ran across the bridge first. Middle Billy Goat Gruff was the next to cross the bridge. He was so big that his feet made a lot of noise when he walked across the bridge. Just as he reached the end of the bridge, a troll jumped up and scared him!		

© 2000 by Linda Hoyt from *Snapshots*. Portsmouth, NH: Heinemann.

Additional Activities for Learning Common Words

The quest for recognition of common words might include:

- Books with cumulative, repetitive structures built around concepts.
- Books that utilize concept words such as *over, under,* and *through* provide natural and meaningful opportunities to heighten awareness of sight vocabulary.
- Traditional favorites such as *Rosie's Walk* by Pat Hutchins, *My Bike* by Craig Martin, *The Bus Ride* published by Celebration Press, *There Were Ten in the Bed, The Chick and the Duckling* by Mirra Ginsburg, and so on all give gently guided repetition of concept words.

Innovations of Favorite Stories

When a child writes a word, the smaller points of letter order and configuration are more likely to be remembered. Also, when these high-frequency words appear in multiple contexts (student writing as well as professional publications), students have support in developing notions of constancy that will assist long-term memory. Innovations of *Rosie's Walk* by Pat Hutchins, for example, often turn into examples like:

ANGELA'S WALK

Angela walked all around the school.

She went

under the sign

over the teeter totter

around the swings

through the gym

and into the classroom.

Cut-up Sentences

When students cut up sentences and reassemble them, they must look closely at individual words while focusing on maintenance of meaning. In *Angela's Walk,* shown above, removing the high-frequency words such as *under, around, through,* etc. provides a rich opportunity for discussion, practice, and yet more creativity as they are reinserted into the text.

Cloze Activities

Example: Innovation on *The Snow* by John Burningham.

One _____ it snowed. Mommy _____ I rolled a big snowball. We _____ a snowman! Then Mommy pulled me _____ a sled. But I fell _____. I lost my glove and I _____ cold. So we _____ indoors. I hope the snow is _____ tomorrow.

Innovation for _The Snow_
by John Burningham

One _____ it snowed. Mommy

_____ I rolled a big snowball. We

_____ a snowman! Then Mommy

pulled me _____ a sled. But I fell

_____. I lost my glove and I

_____ cold. So we _____

indoors. I hope the snow is

_____ tomorrow.

© 2000 by Linda Hoyt from _Snapshots_. Portsmouth, NH: Heinemann.

6

. . . .

Minilessons for Guided Reading and Literature Discussion

It has been exciting over the last few years to watch small-group instruction once again take its place in literacy learning classrooms. Small-group instruction provides special opportunities to observe learners closely and to get to know them better as learners and as individuals. It is also a time when we can "hold the bicycle seat" for those who are wobbling their way through new challenges in text and ensure that their experience is both positive and strategic. If we believe that children are individuals, with individual learning needs, we have an obligation to look beyond whole-class instruction (Traill, 1999) and search for the small-group and individual teaching strategies that enable us to raise the bar for the children and ourselves.

Whether the groups are homogeneous or heterogeneous, small groups increase engagement and provide a critical role in supporting learner development through:

- focusing on individual needs
- explicit teaching
- teacher coaching and scaffolding
- offering strategic support in materials that might be too difficult for independent reading
- social interaction

In the "Schools That Beat the Odds" study (Pearson and Taylor, 1999) it was found that in the most effective classrooms, students were engaged in various small-group experiences for as much as sixty minutes a day. These small groups might emphasize structures such as guided reading, literature circles, reciprocal teaching, or shared book experience

FIGURE 6.1 Linda Hoyt with a small group.

with a small-group. Small-group learning moments could also be increased through partner activities and cooperative learning across the curriculum. Above all, the emphasis is on looking closely at students as individuals and planning instruction to match their specific needs.

To free ourselves to work with small groups, classroom management and meaningful independent work becomes a key factor. As I reflect on this topic, I think of Lucy Calkins (1998) and her caution that we need to put more reading in the reading curriculum. In my own teaching I went through a time where I felt students needed to DO something after they read a book and I had them spend copious numbers of hours coming up with cute responses to literature. During the time I called reading, students were often seen creating dioramas and art projects related to text but doing very little reading. My intentions had been good. My activities did help the children feel good about books, but I should never have called the time "reading."

When children finish a book, the best response is often: Which book will you read next? Will it be another on the same topic? By the same author? or ? The time children spend reading is critical to their development (Allington, 1999) so searches for meaningful and independent activities must hold this notion as the central focus.

Kidshop

While there are many formats and labels for a reading workshop, I like to use the term Kidshop—a term coined by a literacy consultant and wonderful friend from Idaho, Jodi Wilson. I like this format because it keeps children focused on reading (rather than reading-related activity), it involves making choices, and it integrates very well with guided reading, literature circles, and reciprocal teaching formats.

Kidshop is divided into three parts:

- **Minilesson**

The Kidshop opening minilesson is usually a process minilesson. It might focus on remembering to speak quietly, problem solving without interrupting the teacher, making choices from the Kidshop chart, partner reading, using the Listening Center and following along in a book, creating a readers theater straight from the text, and so on.

- **Reading time** and **small groups**

This is the teacher's opportunity to focus on small groups while the rest of the class is working independently. Each small group opens with a minilesson focused on a teaching point specifically needed by that group.

Organizational Format #1   The students make selections from a list of reading options as described below.

Organizational Format #2   Students do not use a list of reading options. They rotate at a signal through predesigned literacy stations with the teacher's small group being one station.

- **Reflection**

Kidshop ends with time to talk about the process. How did it go? Is there anything else we might try? What did we do well? What can we do better? Who can share an example of a problem you solved all alone? Did anyone prepare a poem, special reading, or a reflection to share with the group?

Preparing for Kidshop

In preparing for Kidshop, the students need to understand that everyone has an important job.

THE TEACHER'S JOB	THE STUDENTS' JOB
Present minilessons 　1 to open Kidshop 　1 to each small group	
	Engage in meaningful time with text
Work with small groups	Be independent

To ensure that students have meaningful options, a T-chart of activities is created and continually modified. The teacher fills out the teacher column and asks students for suggestions to list on the student side of the chart. As children make suggestions for the student side of the chart, they are often asked: How will that help you as a reader? How will it help you improve your reading?

The chart is revised often to reflect changes in small groups and to create variety in the list of student options.

The following is a sample T-chart:

TEACHER	STUDENTS (select from this list)
Minilessons	*1. Read a book you love
Group 1	2. Read to a partner
Anna	3. Listen and read along at the listening center
Jose	4. Work with a partner/group to prepare a readers theater presentation
Monro	
Celia	5. Make an audiotape of a favorite book
	*6. Choose one of the word work centers (see the chapter on word awareness)
	Magnetic letters on the overhead
Group 2	Making words with mini pocket charts
Neal	Word wall alphabetizing
Josh	Pocket chart scramble
Delia	7. Read poetry books
Chandra	8. Find a favorite poem and prepare a read aloud
Felicia	9. Write a new version of a favorite book
	10. Read the newspaper
	11. Read a student-authored book
	12. Read several books by the same author
	13. Read several books on the same topic
	14. Practice, then sign up to read to someone in another class
	15. Use the magic pointer to "read the room"

The student activities are numbered so that anytime the noise level becomes a problem, the teacher can ask students to: "Look at the Kidshop Chart. Show me with your fingers the number for the reading work you are doing right now." This usually brings students quickly back on task and the Kidshop continues. Numbers 1 and 6 are required every day for primary students.

Jodi Wilson advocates identifying two students each day as "Teachers" for Kidshop. These students are awarded a special sign for their desk that says: **Teacher**. The other students know that if they have a problem, they go to one of the two "Teachers" for the day and together they make every effort to solve the problem without interrupting the small-group reading time.

The following template for the T-chart might be used to answer several questions:

- What can everyone do to help the Kidshop work well?
- What do we need to be able to concentrate? What can the teacher do to help the students? What can the students do to help the teacher?
- What can the teacher and the students do to solve problems without interrupting each other?
- What is going really well from each perspective? What should we be sure we continue to do?
- What do you need to do your best work as a teacher; as a student? or, as in the sample above, what are our options during Kidshop?

Key Question for Teachers

- How can we structure for independence AND increase time with text?

Key Question for Students

- What are the options for reading that I can handle all by myself?

Creating a T-Chart for Kidshop

THE TEACHER	THE STUDENTS

© 2000 by Linda Hoyt from *Snapshots*. Portsmouth, NH: Heinemann.

Minilessons with Literature Discussion Groups

Literature circles (Daniels, 1994; Schlick Noe and Johnson, 1999) are energizing opportunities for students to engage in authentic conversations about text. They provide small-group discussions that assist learners in looking more deeply at meaning and the author's craft. While literature circles provide for both extensive and intensive reading, I am concerned that in some situations, students are not receiving instruction in reading strategies. As a result, I use a minilesson at either the opening or closing of each literature circle to focus the readers' attention on reading strategies and to maintain a balance between strategic, problem-solving reading (please see Chapter 2 on reading strategies) and the evaluative, connection-building reading that is naturally enhanced within the structure of the literature circle.

Please also see *Revisit, Reflect, Retell* (Hoyt 1999), Chapter 1: Conversations About Books for a wide array of conversation-stimulating activities for before, during, and after reading.

The following assessment tool is designed to assist teachers in assessing reader development for strategic, problem-solving behaviors as well as participation in the deep discussions of a literature circle. With the information gained from such an assessment, minilessons for individual literature circle groups can be targeted directly to the needs of that group of readers. The form itself can be completed by a student and used as a self-reflection and/or by the teacher as a data-gathering source to inform planning of minilessons. I do provide a minilesson on the form itself so that students will understand the target behaviors they need to display to score well either in self-reflection or in a teacher observation.

FIGURE 6.2 Grade two literature circle.

Profile of Reading Development

Fluent Reader Version

Name of Reader _____ Date _____ Text Selection _____

Rating completed by ( ) Reader: Read a passage quietly to yourself

                          ( ) Teacher: Listen to the student read a passage

Reading Strategy Use

	CLEARLY USED			NOT USED	
Before reading:					
Previewed text before reading	5	4	3	2	1
Consciously activated background knowledge	5	4	3	2	1
Made predictions	5	4	3	2	1
Established personal questions for the reading	5	4	3	2	1
During reading:					
Dealt with challenges in text by:					
Reading on to gain context	5	4	3	2	1
Backtracking to regain momentum	5	4	3	2	1
Chunking unknown words	5	4	3	2	1
Making meaningful substitutions	5	4	3	2	1
Self-correcting	5	4	3	2	1
Rate was appropriate to this text	5	4	3	2	1

Continues

© 2000 by Linda Hoyt from *Snapshots*. Portsmouth, NH: Heinemann.

Profile of Reading Development *continued*

After reading:

	CLEARLY USED			NOT USED	
Literature circle observation:					
Is prepared for discussion	5	4	3	2	1
Used the text to support and clarify points	5	4	3	2	1
Made inferences beyond the text	5	4	3	2	1
Made connections	5	4	3	2	1
Used eye contact and active listening behaviors	5	4	3	2	1
Referred to the author's craft	5	4	3	2	1

Notes:

Particular strengths of this reader/discussion participant: _____

_____

_____

_____

_____

Goals/instructional implications for minilessons: _____

_____

_____

_____

© 2000 by Linda Hoyt from *Snapshots*. Portsmouth, NH: Heinemann.

Profile of Reading Development

Emergent Reader Version

Name of Reader _____ Date _____

Text Selection _____

Rating completed by ( ) Reader: Read a passage quietly to yourself
                    ( ) Teacher: Listen to the student read a passage

Before reading:

I look at the pictures	☺	😐	☹
I think: What do I already know?	☺	😐	☹
I predict	☺	😐	☹

During reading:

I think about making sense	☺	😐	☹
I look at the pictures	☺	😐	☹
I look at the beginning and ending	☺	😐	☹
I look for little words in big words	☺	😐	☹
I read on to finish sentences	☺	😐	☹

After reading:

Literature circle observation:

I can tell what the story was about	☺	😐	☹
I talk about the story with my partners	☺	😐	☹
I use examples from the story	☺	😐	☹
I make connections to my life	☺	😐	☹
I make connections to what I know	☺	😐	☹
I ask questions	☺	😐	☹

I am getting really good at _____

I want to get better at _____

Teacher: Instructional implications for minilessons _____

_____

© 2000 by Linda Hoyt from *Snapshots*. Portsmouth, NH: Heinemann.

Literature Circle Poems

For this minilesson, I have the students list the characteristics of a really good literature circle. In some cases I use a T-chart and have the students discuss what a literature circle should look like and sound like:

LOOKS LIKE	SOUNDS LIKE
Leaning in	Only one person talking
Eye contact	Respectful
Looking back in book	Justifying opinions
and so on	

Then we convert their observations to poems about literature circles. They love to perform the poems for each other and post them as charts in the room to remind everyone of the attributes of a literature circles.

Examples:

Lit circle	Flipping through pages
No interruptions	Asking our questions
Eye contact	Supporting our friends
Real questions	Learning from literature circles
Lit circle	

Key Questions

- What makes a literature circle work well?
- How can we remind ourselves of the elements of a high-quality discussion?

Discussion Starters and Stoppers

Students need to understand that some questions and statements stimulate conversation, others bring it to a halt. To stimulate a conversation about discussion, I like to read a thought-provoking selection and then ask a question with a right/wrong answer. The students then decide: Is that question a *starter* or a *stopper*? and Could it stimulate a conversation? We continue the process as the students generate questions about the text and in every case decide if the question is a "starter" or a "stopper."

Sample

Starter or stopper?

Does it give you something to think about and talk about?

QUESTIONS	STARTER?	STOPPER?
Where did this story take place?		
What happened?		
What was your favorite part?		
What did you think of the ending?		
What do you wonder?		
How did it make you feel?		

Really Terrific Questions Chart

From their evaluation of starters and stoppers, we can now start a class chart of Really Terrific Questions! To qualify for inclusion on this chart, a question must work with more than one book and be a sure-fire conversation starter. I find it is best not to laminate the chart so that questions can be added or deleted as the literature circle members develop sophistication.

Stems to Start a Discussion Chart

After reading a selection, I demonstrate making a statement using a stem such as the ones on the following chart, then invite group members to contribute their thoughts using the same stem. I find that the stems are well received by the students and are especially supportive of students who may be hesitant to express themselves.

Key Questions

- What can I say that encourages conversation in my group?
- Which statements and questions help my group to talk about books?
- How can I help my group to look deeply at the story?
- Can I create connections for myself and my group?
- Can I justify my opinions with examples from the book?

Stems to Start a Discussion

I wonder . . .

A connection is . . .

I realized . . .

I think . . .

I wish I could . . .

The story made me think of . . .

If I could change . . .

I noticed . . .

I liked . . .

I feel . . .

I predict . . .

If I could change . . .

My favorite part . . .

What if . . .

My question is . . .

© 2000 by Linda Hoyt from *Snapshots*. Portsmouth, NH: Heinemann.

Memorable Moments

Reader _____

Before I read the story, I anticipated that a memorable moment would be _____

_____ .

As I finished the story, I realized the most memorable moment was _____

_____ .

Another moment that was worthy of attention was

_____

_____ .

I have selected the following quote as an example of how the author created the memorable moment: Page Number _____

_____

_____

_____

_____

© 2000 by Linda Hoyt from *Snapshots*. Portsmouth, NH: Heinemann.

Justifying My Opinions

Author _____   Reader _____

Title _____

The focus: ( ) The book as a whole
                ( ) A character
                ( ) The author's style
                ( ) Other

In each blank below, list a describing word that reflects your focus on the text. This might be three words to describe the book as a whole, three words to describe a character, or three words to describe the author's style. Justify your opinions with specific examples and/or page numbers from the story.

DESCRIBING WORDS   JUSTIFICATION

1. _____   _____

                                                  _____

                                                  _____

2. _____   _____

                                                  _____

                                                  _____

3. _____   _____

                                                  _____

                                                  _____

© 2000 by Linda Hoyt from *Snapshots*. Portsmouth, NH: Heinemann.

Making Connections

Reader _____ Focus Book _____

Good readers think about connections while they read. They think about connections between the book and things they already knew. They make connections between the book and personal experiences. They also make connections between this book and others they may have read.

During reading, stop occasionally and reflect: What connections can I make?

	Connections
What did I already know about the world that I am using during reading today?	
Does this remind me of any experiences I have had?	
Does this remind me of any other books?	

Connections I want to share with my group _____

_____

_____

_____

© 2000 by Linda Hoyt from *Snapshots*. Portsmouth, NH: Heinemann.

Pencils In!

Sometimes groups need support to ensure that all members take responsibility for making contributions to the discussion as well as protecting the group from being monopolized by a particularly verbal group member.

The Only Rule

There is only one rule. You must place your pencil in the center of our circle when you make a contribution to the discussion. You cannot make another contribution until all the pencils are in the center. When all the pencils are in, participants who contribute remove their pencil and wait until all are out before taking another turn.

This really helps reticent students take responsibility for making contributions and is a nonthreatening way to help very verbal students learn the important social skill of turn taking.

It is always interesting to see how long it takes before groups begin to self-regulate and can suspend using their pencils.

If I have multiple groups that would benefit from this strategy, I demonstrate it as a fishbowl so that I sit on the floor with four or five students conducting a real literature discussion and the other observers are circled behind us.

Key Questions

- Am I making a significant contribution to my group?
- Am I taking turns and being an active listener?

Question It

For this snapshot, I use four 2″ × 2″ sticky notes with large question marks on each. I explain to the students that good readers are continually asking themselves questions while they read and that my goal today is to find at least four points in the book where I can ask myself a question.

Demonstrating a Think Aloud

I do a brief think aloud and show them how I could mark a place in the text where I have an "I Wonder" question. I also take a moment to "jot my thoughts" on the back of the sticky note so I can remember my question later.

As I continue my think aloud, I stop often to reflect on whether or not I have a question. Each time I try to demonstrate a different type of question to ask myself. I might model a question I would like to ask the author, a question about the title, how the story might end or what might happen to a character, a question about a conflict between my prior knowledge and something in the story, and so on.

At the end of the think aloud, I show the group how I reflect on my personal questions and select one that might be interesting to share.

Key Questions

- How can I remind myself to ask questions when I read?
- How can I tie my personal questions to our group discussions?
- Could my personal questions stimulate more conversation in our group?

FIGURE 6.3 Question It.

Literature Circles with the Newspaper

Literature circles can often develop a narrow focus on fiction so I consciously insert opportunities for the groups to interact with interesting news articles and other expository sources.

Format

Their interaction with the text could be informal and based on Discussion Stems or Question It from earlier in this chapter, or utilize assigned roles such as Discussion Director, Illustrator, Connector, Passage Picker (Daniels, 1994).

The goal is to create discussions about current events and the strategy shifts that occur when you are reading expository text.

Resources

Other good resources for expository discussions include magazines such as *Ranger Rick*, *World*, *Your Big Backyard*, *Time for Kids*, *Weekly Reader*, and *Sports Illustrated for Kids*.

Key Questions

- Do we need different reading strategies to read a newspaper than a story?
- Do we need different discussion strategies?
- Is a news article worthy of discussion?
- Could the strategies I have learned in literature circles help in other kinds of reading?

News Article for the Overhead

Born of a tough country

When an Eastern Oregon 13-year-old lost his arm in a farm accident, he did something extraordinary

By TOM HALLMAN JR.
THE OREGONIAN

CRANE —

Michael Adams fumbles a bit with his left hand before opening the car door and sliding into the front seat. He frowns slightly when he realizes he can't shake hands with a right arm that, for now, is useless.

He was raised, though, to be polite. So the 13-year-old nods, touches the brim of a white baseball cap smashed down over red hair and flashes a smile to reveal a mouth full of braces.

"Want to see where it happened?" he asks. "I haven't been back there since that day, but I'm ready to see it. Really, I am."

He points to a field about a mile away from his school, the biggest building in Crane, a town nearly 130 miles southeast of Bend, then settles into the seat while the car bounces out of town.

In a farming community where accidents are commonplace, what happened to Michael on July 17 still makes grown men twinge. He was moving an irrigation line when a set of moving gears snagged his sleeve. The machinery cut off his right arm at the shoulder.

What happened next stunned everyone who heard about it: The boy picked up his arm and went two miles for help. That afternoon, the arm was surgically reattached in a Portland hospital.

The extraordinary incident attracted attention from across the country, and interview requests besieged the family. But the Adamses are a private bunch, and they shunned the attention. They went back to Crane so their son could heal in private.

Months passed before they felt Michael was ready to reveal exactly what happened on that terrible day in July.

Please see **BOY,** Page A10

L.E. BASKOW/THE OREGONIAN

Michael Adams studies a field irrigation machine like the one that snagged his jacket in July and cut off his right arm.

INSIDE

Copyright © 1999,
Oregonian Publishing Co.
Vol. 150, No. 50,015
286 pages

An Oregon Century

The two-week series resumes Monday with the 1950s, when Cedar Hills and its resident Mrs. America reflect the decade of a postwar baby boom with one-story starter homes, televisions and low-cost loans for newlyweds.

FIGURE 6.4 *The Oregonian* news article.

© 2000 by Linda Hoyt from *Snapshots*. Portsmouth, NH: Heinemann.

Minilessons for Guided Reading

I like to use two minilesson in each guided reading group: One on a reading strategy or concept of print before reading and one on word awareness strategies during language study at the end of the lesson. During re-reading and independent interactions with the guided reading books, I can gather data on how the children are using the print. This gives me essential information to use in planning minilessons that are directly targeted to learning needs. A guided reading lesson might look something like the following:

A Sample Guided Reading Lesson

Group size: six or less

	INDEPENDENT	TEACHER DIRECTED
Warm Up: Re-reading of a familiar book while the teacher observes and completes a reading profile (see Chapter 2 on strategies)	X	
Picture Walk: The teacher guides a conversation as the students look at the pictures, anticipate vocabulary, activate prior knowledge, and use the language of the text in their conversation		X
Minilesson 1 on a reading strategy or concept of print		X
Independent Reading of Text (Teacher listens to individuals and provides strategy coaching. This is another opportunity to gather running records.)	X	
Re-reading for Fluency Independently or with partners		X
Reflection on Reading Debrief minilesson #1. How did it go? Retelling of story		X
Language Study Minilesson #2: Word practice using magnetic letters, wipe-off boards, literacy frames, cut-up sentences, and so on.		X

Matching Pictures and Text

1. Using a transparency of the pictures on the following page, guide the children through a conversation about each picture, attempting to elicit the language of the text. Ask questions such as: What is happening? What words might you expect to see on this page? and so on. These types of questions may help the students to naturally utilize the vocabulary orally before they will approach it in print.

2. Ask the group to predict two key words for each picture. As the children predict each key word, engage them in predicting the letters in each word.

3. Pass out photocopies of the sentences that match each picture and ask the students to decide which sentences and pictures go together.

4. Look at the key words the students listed and determine if their key words actually appeared in each sentence.

Key Questions

- How do pictures help readers?
- What can readers do to help themselves predict words?
- Good readers make sense. How can the picture help you make sense during reading?

FIGURE 6.5 Picture/word match.

Matching Pictures and Text

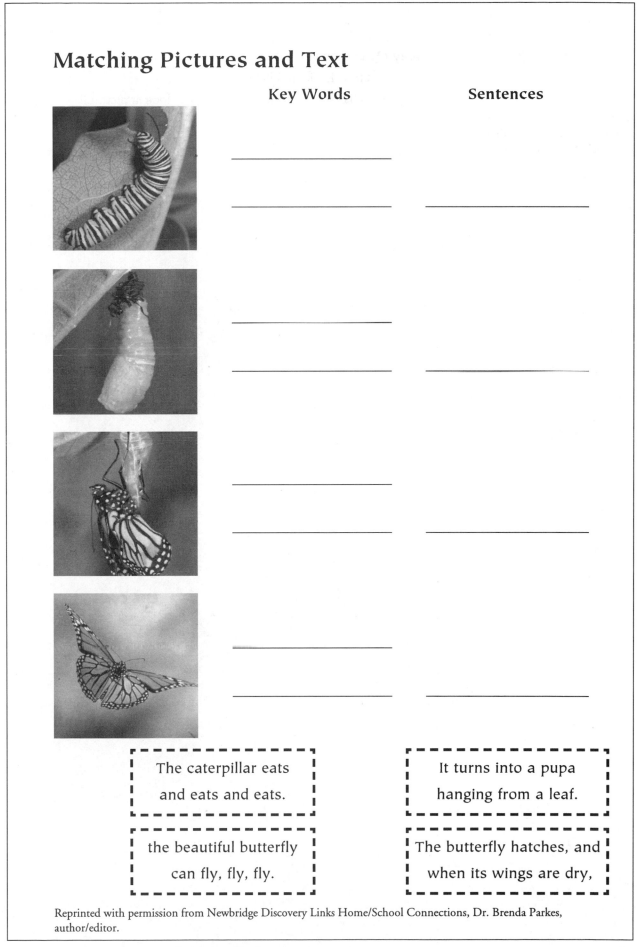

Key Words   Sentences

The caterpillar eats
and eats and eats.

the beautiful butterfly
can fly, fly, fly.

It turns into a pupa
hanging from a leaf.

The butterfly hatches, and
when its wings are dry,

Reprinted with permission from Newbridge Discovery Links Home/School Connections, Dr. Brenda Parkes, author/editor.

© 2000 by Linda Hoyt from *Snapshots*. Portsmouth, NH: Heinemann.

Key Questions

- How do pictures help readers?
- What should readers do when they look at pictures?

Pictures Make a Big Difference

Provide the children with individual copies of *Mrs. Wishy-Washy* by Joy Cowley (Wright Group). Ask the children to "picture walk" through the pages, talking about the storyline and what they think is stated on each page. They may even want to predict a word or two suggested by the pictures on each page.

Once the children reach a phase of feeling very comfortable with the text, replace their books with the text-only version of *Mrs. Wishy-Washy* that follows and ask them to read it.

Support them by talking about how this reading of the text feels. How is it different? The words are the same. What role do the pictures play in our reading? What could be done to make this easier? Knowing that pictures help, can they get pictures in their head to assist their reading?

Key Questions

- How can pictures assist our reading?
- What can I do to remind myself to create pictures in my head?
- Am I using the pictures to help me make sense when I read?

MRS. WISHY-WASHY

In went the cow, wishy-washy, wishy-washy. In went the pig, wishy-washy, wishy-washy. In went the duck, wishy-washy, wishy-washy.

"That's better," said Mrs. Wishy-washy, and she went into the house.

Away went the cow. Away went the pig. Away went the duck.

"Oh, lovely mud," they said.

Reprinted with permission from *Mrs. Wishy-Washy* (1980), by Joy Cowley, Bothell, WA: The Wright Group.

 © 2000 by Linda Hoyt from *Snapshots*. Portsmouth, NH: Heinemann.

Cut-up Sentences and Mini Pocket Charts

Copy a key sentence or two from a familiar guided reading selection, taking care to arrange the words just as they were in the original text. For example, place the return sweep after the same word as in the original text.

Using a sentence from the Matching Pictures and Text snapshot on page 149, I might select:

It turns into a pupa
hanging from a leaf.

Notice how the return sweep occurs after *pupa,* just as in the original text even though I had enough room to have continued the sentence across the line.

After re-reading the familiar book, I ask the student to take scissors and cut the words apart. This allows me to assess understanding of "wordness" and spaces between words. Once the words are separated, I encourage the students to mix up their words and then try to make them into a sentence again. As they work to rebuild the sentence, I can ask questions such as: How do you know which word comes first? What are your clues? How do you know where the ending will be? Which word would make sense next? and so on. Once the sentences are assembled, I refer the children to the original book so they can check their work and see how they did.

As they mature in their reading development, I might ask them to pull the three most important words from their sentence (to focus on key words) and then ask them to use their scissors to cut off the first or last letter from each of those key words. Now, as the words and letters are scrambled, they are going to have to use initial sound cues as well as meaning cues.

At this point, it is very helpful to have a mini pocket chart to control the small pieces. I like the pocket charts that are available at the post office for stamp collectors. They cost around $.65 a piece for the version with five lines per page. With these mini pocket charts, students can manipulate text without worrying that their pieces will be blown away. I also like the idea that if time becomes an issue, it is easy to stop in the middle of rebuilding a sentence and to know the pocket chart is holding everything together so you can continue later.

FIGURE 6.7 Mini pocket charts can be purchased at the post office or coin and stamp collecting shops.

Acetate Overlays

Word searching can bring a wonderful awareness for children as they interact with their guided reading books during language study. They like to search for words with a particular beginning sound, words with a short *o*, adjectives, capitol letters, and so on. (The literacy frames described in the chapter on independent reading can be very helpful for these word searches.)

I also like to purchase acetate by the yard at fabric stores and then cut it to the size of guided reading books. I purchase the heavy acetate so it can withstand a lot of handling over time.

During the language study portion of guided reading, I pass out acetate sheets and overhead markers, then send the students on word searches in their books. When they find a word with a particular phonemic principle, they circle it and share it with the group. For some students, tracing the word and reading it to the group is a helpful way to practice letter formation and reinforce spelling patterns. Students working on the same phonemic element enjoy making a chart of words to demonstrate the same pattern and posting it on the walls of the classroom.

Variations

- Rebuild story words with a particular pattern using magnetic letters. Place the magnetic letters on the overhead projector.
- Use Wikki Stix (Omnicor, Inc. Phoenix, Arizona) to frame words.

FIGURE 6.8 Acetate.

FIGURE 6.9 Magnetic letters.

FIGURE 6.10 Wikki Stix.

Key Questions

- What do we know about sentences?
- What helps us know what words come next?

Trick Me!

Children really enjoy surprising each other so I take advantage of that natural response with the Trick Me! strategy. At the end of guided reading, I tell them that we are going to play a game and try to trick each other. One student will be the Trickster and one will be the Reader.

The Trickster's job is to place a sticky note over a word in our story then hand their guided reading book to the Reader. The Reader reads the story and tries to guess which word is hiding under the sticky note.

I coach the Tricksters to try to hold back and not tell if the word is correct but instead to ask questions just like a teacher:

> Does it make sense?
> What makes you think it is that word?
> Are there any other words that might work?

Then, the Trickster and the Reader can remove the sticky note and do it again.

Variations
- Tell the children to cover a word EXCEPT for its beginning sound.
- Cover a word EXCEPT for its ending sound.
- Ask the Reader to predict TWO words that make sense. Then the Trickster moves the sticky note slightly aside to uncover the beginning sound and the Reader needs to predict other letters that might be in the word.

Key Questions
- How do readers know what words come next, even when they can't SEE the word?
- What should good readers do when they read?

Strategy Glove

To assist readers in remembering to use a wide range of strategies while reading, I make Strategy Gloves to remind them of their options.

Introducing the Gloves

During a minilesson on strategies for guided reading, I introduce the glove and work with the students to talk through the range of strategies they are currently using. I then present each student with a strategy glove to wear during the independent reading portion of the lesson. The goal is to refer to the glove when they come to a challenge in their reading and to remember to use *many* strategies, not just one to help themselves.

The gloves are white gardener's gloves that can be purchased at any garden department. I write strategies on the glove that developmentally match a group of students so I eventually collect a wide range of gloves with different strategies represented.

Other Options

A money-saving option is to use plastic food handlers gloves. These are very inexpensive and disposable after a few reading lessons. Plastic food handlers gloves are also a great option for sharing this strategy with parents and providing them with Strategy Gloves to use at home.

Key Questions

- Which strategies do I use the most?
- Which strategies should I try to use more often?
- If I made a list of strategies, how long would it be?

FIGURE 6.11 Strategy Glove.

Partner Retells

For this minilesson, I need a guided reading book that is familiar to the group and a child, the Storyteller, who knows the story well enough to retell it.

Telling the Story

While the Storyteller tells the story, the group members listen carefully. At the end of the telling, the group members go through their guided reading books slowly and place a sticky note on any pages that the Storyteller described in the retell.

Next, group members compliment the Storyteller on the parts of the story that were included with a statement such as: "I noticed you included _____."

An additional step that could be added would be to provide clues about story elements the Storyteller did not remember to include in the retell. Group members provide clues and the Storyteller pages through the book as a support to including the missing elements.

FIGURE 6.12 Partner retells.

FIGURE 6.13 Retell with fifth graders.

Partner Groupings

Once the students catch on, I ask them to meet with a partner and agree who will be the Storyteller and who will be the Listener. They re-read the story independently and think about the key elements. Then, the Storyteller proceeds as above while the listener places sticky notes on the pages that were included in the retell.

See *Revisit, Reflect, Retell* (Hoyt, 1999), Chapters 1 and 2 for many more ideas on oral retelling with narrative texts.

Prompts for Teachers to Support
Reading Strategies

Concepts About Print
Where do you start reading?
Put your finger on the first word.
Which way are you going?
Can you find the title?

Meaning Cues
Did that make sense?
How could the pictures help you?
What do you think might happen next?
What do you know in your head about ___ that might help you here?

Structure Cues
Did that sound like the way we talk?
Can you say it another way?
Is there another word that might work here?

Visual Cues
Were there enough words on that line to match what you said?
Can you point to . . . ?
What letters do you think will be in that word?
How did you know that word was ___?
Look at the beginning . . . at the ending.
Are there any little words in this word?
Get your mouth ready to say the word ____.

Cross-Checking/Self-Monitoring
How did you know?
Show me . . . what makes you think so?
It could be that . . . if you look again and think . . . could it be anything else?
Why don't you re-read and check it.
Were you right?
What did you notice?

© 2000 by Linda Hoyt from *Snapshots*. Portsmouth, NH: Heinemann.

7

Independent Reading
Personalizing the Learning
in Books I Choose Myself

Time to read the books that you select yourself is essential to developing a positive attitude about reading and understanding that it is a deeply personal act that is useful throughout life. One of the literacy mistakes I made in raising my three children was waiting until after they were in bed to offer myself the reward of reading the newspaper or picking up a novel. While I was meticulous about reading to my children, I neglected to demonstrate that reading brought me personal pleasure. As those children have grown, I have had the sad opportunity of watching them read less and less. As college students, they are so embattled with mandatory reading assignments that they seem to have forgotten that personal reading can bring pleasure, relief from stress, and the opportunity to explore issues of personal interest. They have lost touch with reading for personal purposes and as a result have a diminished set of reading strategies that now include mostly skim, scan, and find the answer strategies.

The research is very clear about the power of independent reading. The task for teachers is to stand strong in support of its value and allocate substantial amounts of time to independent reading every day. Anderson, Wilson, and Fielding (1988) reported that time spent reading books is the best predictor of reading achievement in students in second through fifth grade. Students in fourth through twelfth grades who reported doing more daily reading at school and home reported higher average scores on standardized tests than those who did not (National Center for Education Statistics, 1999; McQuillan, 1998). Lucy Calkins, along with her writing partners Montgomery and Santman (1998), remind us that most standardized tests of reading comprehension for third graders take

FIGURE 7.1 Student reading independently.

sixty to seventy minutes to complete, yet the average third grader in the United States is reading less than fifteen minutes per day. They go on to suggest that we need to put more reading in the reading curriculum to build the stamina children need to be able to spend longer blocks of time reading independently.

We must communicate the value of independent reading to parents, administrators, and the children themselves. We need to assure ourselves and those who observe our practices that independent reading is worthy of substantial time allocations in school. Some teachers worry that independent reading time looks like no one is teaching or that some students may not use the time wisely. These are valid concerns. To deal with those questions we must continue to look to research and remember that the students who read the most are the best readers (National Center for Educational Statistics, 1999) and that students who read for at least twenty minutes a day, every day, have the potential to gain 1,000 new

FIGURE 7.2 Grade two readers.

vocabulary words a year (Nagy, Anderson, and Herman, 1987)—far more than we could teach through direct instruction. In addition, the students are gaining vocabulary by simply reading connected, meaningful texts.

It is helpful to plan for at *least* twenty to thirty minutes every day PLUS one special day every week when the time is lengthened to more closely approximate the attention span demanded by a standardized test. In a recent study entitled, "Schools That Beat the Odds" (1999), P. David Pearson and B. Taylor found that the most effective schools engaged children in independent reading for *not less than* twenty-eight minutes per day even in the primary grades.

Lots of Books and Lots of Time!

It is helpful to have a wide range of texts in the classroom for independent reading. Students need access to good stories, high-quality expository texts, magazines, and books on tape. Allington (1999) and Krashen (1998) suggest that a classroom needs approximately 1,200 books available at all times to support the kind of independent reading experiences that produce committed, self-motivated readers. Also, those classroom collections need to be backed up by well-stocked media centers that are highly accessible to children. While that number of books may sound daunting, many teachers have found that media specialists and pubic librarians can provide assistance in rotating classroom collections and that garage sales, yard sales, and requests for donations can produce surprising results.

When readers expect a lengthy period of independent reading every day, they begin thinking ahead about their book choices, gathering collections of books on related topics, books by a favorite author, and so on. This sense of anticipation and planning mirrors the way many adults handle their personal reading and helps students to understand that reading is something you do for yourself rather than for your teacher. As with writing, predictable periods of independent reading every day encourages children to become committed on a personal level and to establish personal reading as a habit.

Emergent readers need opportunities to be independent even if they are role-play readers (First Steps, 1995). They need to handle books, construct stories from pictures, and let themselves be carried away by wonderful pictures in magazines such as *Your Big Backyard* and *Ranger Rick*. As with all language learning opportunities, emergent readers need to try on the feeling of being fluent and be treated as readers in the fullest sense. When I walk into kindergarten classrooms and watch five-year-olds (sometimes alone and sometimes with partners) fully engaged in independent reading, I know that these learners are being given a treasured gift. They see themselves as readers and are developing confidence in book handling that provides a rich foundation for continued literacy development.

In addition to a rich mix of genres for independent reading, emergent readers need access to books that are familiar favorites. Familiar favorites previously shared during read aloud sessions, shared book experiences, and guided reading provide emergent readers with the needed scaffolding to apply their fledgling strategies in books that are already meaningful. The familiar storylines assist the readers in making meaning while they read and help to avert the potential danger of meaningless word calling. As a result, I try to ensure that the books I read to the students and the books we use in guided reading are easily available for independent reading.

To build stamina for lengthy periods of independent reading and ensure that children make the most of this important time, I try to create systems that keep students reading instead of walking around the room. For those students who have difficulty settling into a book and want to constantly change titles, I work with them to find a number of reasonable titles that are at a comfortable reading level and are of high interest. Then, I arrange to have those books either stacked or in a basket next to the student. With the books close at hand, a change of titles only requires a moment and they are once again reading. Since emergent and role-play readers can finish their small books so quickly, I provide baskets of books on their tables. The objective is to read during independent reading!

What Happens During Independent Reading?

Minilesson   I always open independent reading with a minilesson but I am committed to keeping it very short as the goal is to read and I don't want to use the precious time talking. The minilesson might be on a procedure such as what to do when you finish a book. It might be on a reading strategy, or a structure for building accountability and deepening understanding. My goal is to help students personalize the instruction that has been provided in read alouds, shared book experiences, guided reading, and other teacher-directed structures. Independent reading is the time to implement learning and synthesize the good habits that we know will carry them into life-long engagement with reading.

Reading   After the opening minilesson, I like to start reading a book of my own. Because I am reading, I can fairly explain to the students that they need to read independently so that I can enjoy my own book. I usually try to read for five to eight minutes as a positive demonstration of how sincerely I value this time.

Conferences   Once the students appear to be settling in and engaging with their books, I quietly begin to call students for individual reading conferences. In the "Schools That Beat the Odds" study (Pearson and Taylor, 1999), one of the key factors in schools that had high levels of achievement was the element of "coaching" during reading. This coaching was designed to ensure that readers were supported in developing a wide array of strategies and that the strategies could be applied independently in a variety of texts.

Reflection   The last five to eight minutes of every independent reading period is for reflection. I ask students to bring their reading to a close, mark their places, and get ready to share. This is when we can take the topic of the minilesson and talk to each other about efforts to apply the focus of the minilesson. I believe that this reflection is critical to long-term memory and to helping students actually internalize the strategies I am trying to help them implement. After we debrief the minilesson, I invite students to share memorable moments from the reading time. Were there any books they were particularly excited about? a passage to read aloud and just savor the language of? Or?

Key Questions for Teachers
- How can we provide extensive amounts of independent reading both inside and outside of school?
- How can we communicate about the importance of independent reading to parents, administrators, and students?

Making Independent Reading the Best It Can Be

I start this minilesson by asking students to make a list of the kind of interruptions that might cause them to stop reading during independent reading time.

As you can imagine, they list things like:

- Someone was noisy and bothered me
- I was thirsty
- I finished my book
- I didn't like my book

Next I ask them to make a list of solutions for any of these potential disruptions to the time:

PROBLEM	SOLUTION
Noisy classmate	Make agreements about how to create a quiet environment
Thirsty	Get water right before independent reading
Finished my book	Have baskets of books on tables in a stack in front of a student so no one needs to get up and search for a new book

We then test out their solutions and consider: Was it better? Were you able to pay closer attention to your book? Was it quieter? How did you feel about it? What else could we try to help ourselves spend longer periods of time?

Ultimately, we generate a list of agreements on How to Make Independent Reading the Best It Can Be.

FIGURE 7.3 Grade four students reviewing the list of agreements.

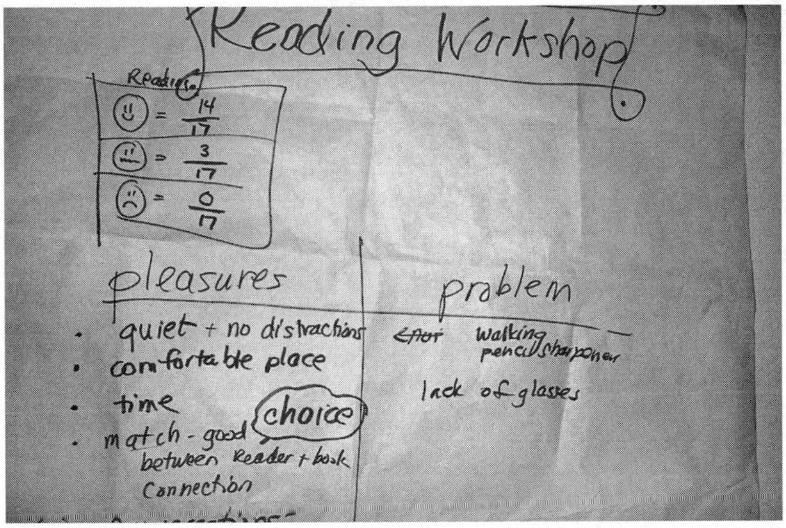

FIGURE 7.4 Chart by Teresa Therriault, Literacy Facilitator, Beaverton, Oregon.

Key Questions

- What can we do to help ourselves lengthen our independent reading times?
- What might we do to help those who need quiet to concentrate?
- What do I learn about reading during independent reading time?
- Am I remembering to use good reader strategies during independent reading time?

Independent Think Alouds

I start this minilesson by modeling a think aloud with the book I am using for my independent reading. I turn pages and in a self-reflective way,

- describe the visual images
- make predictions about what I think may happen
- talk about connections I notice between the text and my experiences
- tell the children about connections between this book and any others I have read

It can also be helpful to have the following transparency on the overhead so I can refer to it during my think aloud and remind myself of key points.

Next, I ask the students to quickly look through the book they are about to read and select two places where they will plan to stop and engage in an "independent think aloud" about their book. Students could mark these places with sticky notes, paper clips, jot down the page numbers, or use whichever strategy seems most appropriate to their development.

I put the transparency from the following page on the overhead and invite the students to read to their first marker, look at the clues on the overhead, and take time for personal reflection before reading on.

At the end of independent reading, students come together to talk about the impact their reflections had on their reading.

Variations

- Have readers draw pictures at each of the two stop points to reflect their visualizations
- Have readers "Jot a Thought" at the stop point and record brief thoughts
- Focus the students on just connections with a three-point grid and ask them to consciously try to make each connection at the stop point

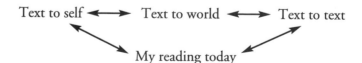

- Jot "I Wonder" questions at the stop point
- At the stop points, refer to the class strategy chart and silently notice strategies you have remembered to use

Key Questions

- Am I applying good reader strategies during my independent reading time?
- How can I help myself remember?
- Am I remembering to visualize?
- Am I making connections as I read?

Independent Think Alouds

 As you reach each stop point in your book, **STOP**, and . . .

 Make a picture in your head: **Visualize**

? Predict

What do you think will happen?

What topic will be addressed next?

Make Connections

Your experiences and the text
This text and another one
This text and something you already knew

© 2000 by Linda Hoyt from *Snapshots*. Portsmouth, NH: Heinemann.

Choosing a Just-Right Book

Book selection has continued to be a challenge for many of the students I work with as well as a key factor in students' ability to sustain attention. As with adults, they will stick with a book for a longer period of time if they really like it and feel comfortable.

Selecting a Book

I start this minilesson by showing the students several picture books and talking about my decision in selecting one. I explain that I look at the pictures, I think about the topic, I think about any other books by the same author, then I read the first page. If the page appeals to me and it makes sense to me, I am ready to make my decision.

Sometimes, I even demonstrate abandoning a book by reading a page or two and explaining that I just didn't like it as much as I thought and then selecting another book.

Listing Strategies

We then list the steps I followed on a chart and I ask the students to add their favorite strategies for selecting a book to read.

During independent reading, students who are choosing books are reminded to try out the suggestions on the list to see how they work and to be ready to report to the group at the end of independent reading.

At the end of reading, students think about successful strategies and make modifications to the class list.

CHOOSING A JUST-RIGHT BOOK

- You need to know a little bit about the topic.
- The book needs to look interesting
- You can read most of the words.
- You read the first page and think:
    Does it make sense?
    Do you like it?
    Does it make you want to read more?

(written by grade two students)

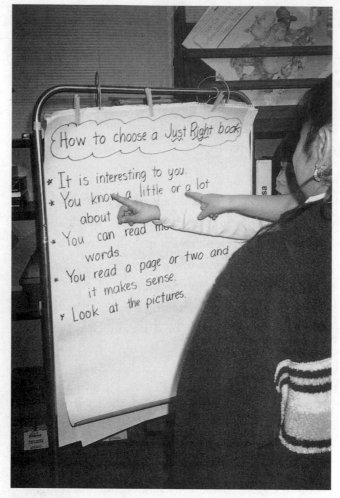

FIGURE 7.5 How to choose a just-right book.

Key Questions

- How can you find a good book?
- What should you look for?
- What should you do if you don't like the book as much as you thought?
- How might you apply the Choosing a Just-Right Book strategies when you are at the library?

Keeping a Genre Log

Students need exposure to varied texts so they can begin to notice the differences in text structures, differences in writing styles, purposes for text, and the subtle strategy shifts that readers employ when they shift genre and purpose.

Read Alouds

Read alouds are a wonderful way to expose children to a wide range of genres. As I read to the students, I try to point out the differences in the texts and encourage them to assist me in thinking about how the structure of the texts is alike and different. For example, students enjoy comparing the differences between a newspaper article and a computer manual. They are both expository texts but have significantly different purposes and structures.

As part of this plan for introducing students to a wide range of texts, I keep a log of the books I share using a form similar to the one on the following page.

Once students catch on, I invite them to make suggestions for texts that we could enjoy during read aloud time and that might be different from others we have encountered so far.

Students' Genre Logs

To personalize the learning and follow through on my plan for a gradual release of responsibility, I have the students start a genre log during small group reading time. Since this is a time when I lead their groups and have a say in text selection, guided reading groups and literature circle groups can record their readings and discuss their observations while I am there to coach. It also helps to assure me that I am not overly relying on one text structure or genre for instruction.

Eventually, I transfer this process to independent reading and ask every children to record in a genre log each time they change texts and make observations about the texts they read.

Sample Genre Log

Text	Date	Genre	The structure: How is it organized? Can you name another text that is alike or different?	Will you choose this again?
Time for Kids	10/22	magazine	This is a lot like Weekly Reader. Pictures and short passages.	Yes
The Far Side	10/17	cartoon	Pictures and short statements. I don't get all of them. I need to work at making connections.	Yes

Key Questions

- What kinds of texts have I spent time reading?
- How are they alike and different?
- Do I notice any relationship between their structures and their purpose?
- Which kinds of texts do I enjoy most?
- What am I learning about types of texts that might help my writing?
- What shifts do I have to make in strategies when I change texts?

Genre Log

Reader_____

Text	Date	Genre	The structure: How is it organized? Can you name another text that is alike or different? Any strategy shifts?	Would you choose this again?
_____	_____	_____	_____	_____
_____	_____	_____	_____	_____
_____	_____	_____	_____	_____
_____	_____	_____	_____	_____
_____	_____	_____	_____	_____
_____	_____	_____	_____	_____
_____	_____	_____	_____	_____
_____	_____	_____	_____	_____
_____	_____	_____	_____	_____
_____	_____	_____	_____	_____
_____	_____	_____	_____	_____
_____	_____	_____	_____	_____
_____	_____	_____	_____	_____

© 2000 by Linda Hoyt from *Snapshots*. Portsmouth, NH: Heinemann.

Book Reviews

Students enjoying hearing the opinions of their peers and are more likely to select a book when it comes with a recommendation from a friend. As a result, I encourage the students to do lots of book reviews for the books they read during independent reading.

Demonstration

I start by demonstrating a book review as a minilesson. I either read professional reviews from the newspaper or write one of my own to give the students an idea of how a book review might sound. I want to make it clear that this is not a retell—it is an *evaluation* of the book. I remind students that this is a little like a commercial. When you watch a commercial on television, its purpose is to sell a product and convince you to buy it. A book review has the same attributes, except that a book reviewer might also tell you NOT to read the book. The important issue is to have an opinion and then justify the opinion with specific information.

Launching the Reviews

I explain that we will be doing book reviews at the end of independent reading. I encourage students to stop reading periodically and to make a conscious effort to think about their review so that they will be fully prepared to share at the end of our reading time. I find that students tend to try a littler harder to connect with their books when they know they will be reviewing for a listener. I also find that for teachers who are concerned about whether or not the students are "really reading" during this time, an end-of-reading review adds a measure of accountability unlike a test or series of teacher-generated questions.

Partner Reviews   Involve pairing students to meet with a partner, having them show the books they are reading, and doing brief reviews for each other. If the students are having trouble getting started, I make an overhead transparency or Review Guidelines card with some reminders. Even a starter as simple as "Say Something" (Harste, Short, and Burke, 1988) can help students get started and frame the book review as a genuine conversation between readers.

Group Reviews   Require that teams of four to six students sit in a circle, and share their book reviews. With the group reviews, I do ask students to jot down their key thoughts as some students get so involved listening that they forget what they had to say about their own book.

Sticky Note Reviews   For this review process, I give each student a 3 × 5 sticky note and encourage them to write their review on the note, sign it, and place it inside the front cover of the book. Soon, many of the classroom books are filled with personal reviews and these play a large role in book selection.

Key Questions

- What are the traits of a good book?
- How are the books I like different from the ones I don't like?
- How can I quickly communicate my opinions to another reader?
- How might my review help another reader?
- How can I be specific and use examples from the book to justify my opinion?

Book Review Guidelines

Book Review Format 1:
Answer the following kinds of questions:

Did you like the book?

Why? Be specific. Show and tell.

Book Review Format 2:
Was there anything about the author's message or style that seemed unique?

Would you recommend it to someone else? Why? Be specific.

Book Review Format 3:
If you were going to write a review of this book to be published in a newspaper, what would you want the readers to know about it?

© 2000 by Linda Hoyt from *Snapshots*. Portsmouth, NH: Heinemann.

Key Words to Summarize

Good readers can summarize and identify main ideas (Keene and Zimmerman, 1997). While many students can summarize with guidance, it is important to give them practice summarizing independently, as that is the mode of reading and thinking that empowers them as independent learners.

I provide students with a photocopy of a paragraph or use a transparency on the overhead. I then enlist their help in identifying the main idea of the passage and a supporting detail or two.

Summaries

Next, I engage in a think aloud describing how I would plan a short summary of the paragraph, showing students how to start, how to decide what to include, what to leave out, and how to avoid just repeating the words of the author. A critical feature of my planning is identifying a key word for each sentence. In my think aloud, I want the students to see that the words sometimes come directly from the text, and sometimes they are a combination of the text and my reaction. I can then use the words to summarize.

EXAMPLE: SUMMARY	KEY WORDS
The power of the crocodile is like that of a monstrous machine. With one lunge it can destroy its prey and protect the kill from other predators. Its powerful tail propels it forward at enormous speed, allowing it to surprise the animal it is stalking. As the huge jaws clamp down and snare the animal, the crocodile buries its head underwater. This action drowns the prey and removes the kill from the view of other predators. In one swift, powerful lunge the crocodile both kills and protects its dinner.	Powerful Protect Fast Underwater Kill/Protect

I ask them to evaluate my summary and decide if I included the most important facts and kept it short enough.

As the students begin independent reading, I explain that they need to select a paragraph from today's reading that they will orally summarize at the end of independent reading. I provide sticky notes so they can identify passages as they read that they want to consider for summarizing.

At the end of independent reading, have students meet in partners to share the passages they have selected and then work with their partner to craft a short summary of the passage. Encourage them to work together to determine the essential elements to include in their oral summaries, even though they were reading different books.

Key Questions

- What are the characteristics of a brief paragraph summary?
- How do you separate main ideas from supporting details?
- How do you keep it short and avoid just repeating the author's words?
- What else might you have tried?

Key Words to Summarize

The Crocodile	Key Words
The power of the crocodile is like that of a monstrous machine. With one lunge it can destroy its prey and protect the kill from other predators. Its powerful tail propels it forward at enormous speed, allowing it to surprise the animal it is stalking. As the huge jaws clamp down and snares the animal, the crocodile buries its head underwater. This action drowns the prey and removes the kill from the view of other predators. In one swift, powerful lunge the crocodile both kills and protects its dinner.	

© 2000 by Linda Hoyt from *Snapshots*. Portsmouth, NH: Heinemann.

Using Personal Literacy Frames

Don Holdaway designed "masks" as devices to assist young children in focusing on key points in text during shared book experiences. Mini versions of these frames can be wonderful tools for supporting reading development through independent reading.

Working with Frames

Provide each student with a literacy frame (see the pattern on the next page) and let them practice framing words in their independent reading books. Depending on the learner's phase of development, he might frame in a word with that starts with *b*, a word with a short *o*, a word with an *ing* ending, an adjective, a word with three syllables, etc. Because the frame slides easily and adjusts to the length of each word, children enjoy the kinesthetic interaction and focus their visual attention easily on the teaching point.

Multiple Uses

I find that these frames are helpful during individual reading conferences, at the end of guided reading, or during the end of reading reflections for independent reading. At the end of independent reading, for example, even though everyone has a different book, I can ask the group to frame words with a particular attribute and show their partners what they found. This provides interaction with multiple examples of the phonemic principle even though all students are reading different books.

I also find that the frames assist me in differentiating curriculum. To accomplish this, I might walk around the room and pass out colored

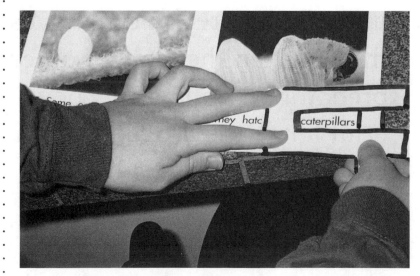

FIGURE 7.6 Practicing with literacy frames.

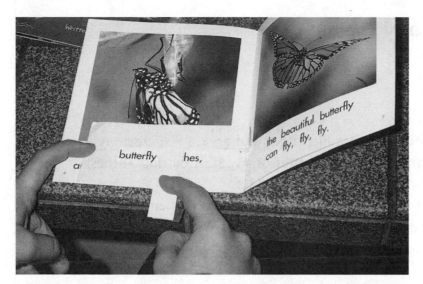

FIGURE 7.7 A student working with literacy frames.

index cards. The students have no idea why I give different students different colors, but I know, and I might say: If you have a red card, frame a three-syllable adjective. If you have a blue card, frame a word with a short vowel, etc. The students then take their independent reading books, meet in groups with others bearing the same color cards, and word search together to find examples in their varied books of words with the same pattern.

Key Questions
- What did you notice about the words you framed?
- Which pattern were you examining?

Pattern for Literacy Frame

Demonstration Size:

1. Starting from the folded edge of a file folder, cut an 8.5 × 6″ rectangle.
2. Remove a 2 × 7″ rectangle from the center of #1. Start cutting at the open edge so the fold remains completely intact.
3. Using the remnants of the file folder, start at the fold and cut a 1-inch wide strip that runs from the fold all the way across the folder.
4. Slide the 1-inch strip over the open ends of the "U"-shaped section and staple as indicated.
5. Slide the thin strip back and forth to adjust the frame to the size of the word or letter you are working on.

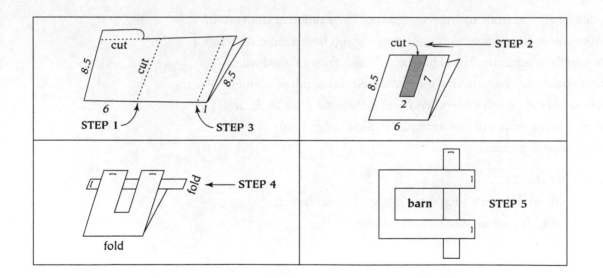

Individual Student Size:

1. Follow the directions above with the following changes in dimension:

   The original rectangle cut from the fold should be 5 × 2″.

   Remove a .75 × 4″ rectangle from the center of the 5 × 2″ segment.

   Cut a strip .5 × 3″ beginning at the fold.

   Staple or tape open edges.

Adapted from Linda Hoyt Seminars (originally by Don Holdaway in large size for big books).

 © 2000 by Linda Hoyt from *Snapshots*. Portsmouth, NH: Heinemann.

Conducting Conferences During Independent Reading

The conferences that occur during independent reading are vitally important to my understanding of my students and their individual needs. During these conferences I can assess their use of the cueing systems, listen to and evaluate retells, and get a better understanding of how instruction might be crafted to support individual learning needs.

The Format

I like to use a format in which one student is "on deck" and sitting three to four feet away while a second student sits with me.

At the "on-deck station," I provide a basket filled with sticky notes and pens. The student at this station knows that she is responsible for preparing a retell and a passage to read orally from the book. The student on deck might mark a favorite passage with the sticky notes or plan to just "read on" from whatever points she is at in the text. Some students like to use the sticky notes to jot down opinions about the book, questions they want to ask, or begin a book review to be left on the sticky note and affixed to the inside cover of the book for their peers to read.

The student who is actively conferencing sits next to me. This student understands that our conference will be brief, perhaps two to four minutes, and that he or she is responsible to lead the way. The student opens the conference with a conversation about the story or a brief retell, and then orally reads a brief passage. The passage may be selected because it was especially meaningful to the student, because the student feels especially good about his or her ability to read it with expression, or because it was a bit confusing. Many students elect to just "read on" from whatever point they are at.

This is a powerful time to privately gather information on the student's depth of understanding of the text by taking anecdotal notes or quickly scoring the retell (see *Revisit, Reflect, Retell,* Hoyt, 1999, pages 62–70). This is also a good time to take a quick running record or do a short-form reading miscue inventory (see Chapter 2 on Strategies). I can then offer congratulations on strategies the reader is using effectively and make suggestions about additional strategies that might be implemented. I try to continually remind myself that this is only one instructional moment and not the entire instructional program, so I keep it brief. I monitor the time and resist the temptation to spend more than two to four minutes with each student.

After the brief conference, the conferencing reader quietly taps the shoulder of the person who will be next on "on deck." The current on-deck student slides into the conference chair and conference #2 begins.

This rotation goes very quickly since the on-deck student has had time to reflect and organize for the conference.

Reading Conferences

Purposes of the Conference
- Assess learner strengths and plan for intentional teaching points
- Provide feedback that will enhance the reader's ability to make use of all cueing systems
- Support strategies that are in place
- Introduce new strategies
- Support and deepen comprehension

The Setting
- Sit next to the student, not across, to create a sense of partnership
- Share a book so you can be a sincere listener
- Encourage the student to talk: What is going well? What assistance might I offer?

The Steps for the Student
- On deck: get ready by planning a retell and selecting a portion for oral reading

The Steps for the Teacher
- Assess the retell for complexity and understanding
- Assess the oral reading for strategic reading behaviors
- Provide feedback
- Select one teaching point

The following are strategies to encourage.

Before Reading
- Predict
- Set purpose
- Activate prior knowledge
- Ask questions

During Reading
- Ask personal questions
- Self-monitor comprehension
    Does this make sense?
    Read on/backtrack
    Self-correct
    Use pictures
    Use letters and word parts

After Reading
- Pull it all together
- What did I read?
- How did I handle my strategies?
- Goals for improvement?

Preparing for a Conference

Preparing to Read Orally

 Think about the book. Was there a part you especially liked or had questions about?

 If so, rehearse reading that part and mark it with sticky notes so you can find it quickly.

 Think about reading strategies. Are there any you can demonstrate while reading?

Preparing Your Retell

 Think about the book.

 What are the most important parts? Important ideas?

 Rehearse in your head. What will you include in your retell? Make sure to keep it short and focused on the most important points.

© 2000 by Linda Hoyt from *Snapshots*. Portsmouth, NH: Heinemann.

Providing Feedback to Readers

WHEN THE CHILD . . .	THE LISTENER/COACH MIGHT . . .
Stops reading.	Ask: "What have you tried?" "What could you try next?" "What are your good reader options?" "Have you checked the picture?" "I wonder about reading on to finish the sentence . . ." "Sometimes rereading helps, let's backtrack and come through again." "Try the beginning and ending sounds." "Are there any word parts that might help you?" "Could you put in a word that makes sense and read on?"
Attempts to sound out but is breaking down.	Suggest: "Why don't you put your finger over the word and think for just a moment." "What would make sense here?" "Now that you have thought of some words that make sense, look at the beginning and ending sounds. Are there any word parts that help you?" "I wonder what words start with ___ and would also sound right in this sentence." "Were you right? How do you know?"
Reads through errors and doesn't seem to notice.	Wait. Give enough time for the child to have a chance to self-correct. If the child finishes a page and still doesn't self-correct, ask for a retell. (Sometimes they are self-correcting in their heads and really do understand.) If the retell is tangled, take the child back into a portion of the text where the reading was still clear and then read on into the trouble spot. Watch carefully for self-corrections from the first reading. If the child does self-correct, offer praise and show the difference between

WHEN THE CHILD . . .	THE LISTENER/COACH MIGHT . . .
	the first and second reading. If the child is using words that do not make sense, stop the reader and explain that as a listener you are feeling like it doesn't make sense. Ask how the child is feeling about it and then work through the text together, placing special emphasis on making sense, sounding like language, and using the visual cues.
Self-corrects independently.	Offer lots of praise! "Way to go!" "How did you know?"
Attempts to self-correct but produces a new miscue.	Praise the attempt then show the visual and meaning cues that were needed.
Finishes.	"Good readers are always trying new ways to help themselves. Today I noticed you tried _____." "Which strategies worked best for you?"

Reading Record for Individual Conferences

Reader Name _____

Book	Date	Strategies Used Today	Teaching Points for Next Time
1. _____	_____	_____	_____
		_____	_____
		_____	_____
2. _____	_____	_____	_____
		_____	_____
		_____	_____
3. _____	_____	_____	_____
		_____	_____
		_____	_____

Watching for:

Predicting   Does it sound right?
Reading on   Does it look right?
Backtracking/re-reading   Self-corrections
Using beginning sounds   Personal connections to text
Using ending sounds   Conscious application of strategies
Chunking   Use of picture clues
Monitoring: Does it make sense?

© 2000 by Linda Hoyt from *Snapshots*. Portsmouth, NH: Heinemann.

8

Informational Text
Strategies for Success in All Content Areas

As I think about the reading I do as an adult, I realize that my life is filled with nonfiction! I read the newspaper, recipes, my grocery list, my list of things to do, the notes from my family members, notes from my colleagues, my e-mail, my computer manual, and so on. It has become a rarity for me to sit down with a novel, a short story, or a book of poetry.

I believe we must engage children at the earliest stages of literacy development with nonfiction reading and writing (Duke, 1999). In an information age where the volume of world knowledge is expanding at such a dramatic rate, we can no longer support the old adage of "learning to read" and then "reading to learn." Children must, from the emergence of literacy, have opportunities to engage with real-world information while they are learning about print. As a result, many educators are calling for an increased emphasis on teaching children the strategies they need to succeed with expository texts from the emergency of literacy (Hoyt, 1999). There is a call to dramatically shift the traditional emphasis on narrative and story in the primary grades and focus on expository texts as core vehicles for reading instruction (Siera and Siera, 1999).

This kind of shift is also supportive of English Language Learners, as informational texts tend to remove cultural barriers and support concept-based translation from one language into another.

When I challenge myself to look objectively at the structure of my literacy program, fortunately I can confirm that children are interacting with nonfiction texts in every single area on a consistent basis. I find that this happens naturally in writing. As children write about their experiences, they naturally use expository forms of expression to tell about real events and people. In reading, however, I must continually step back and ensure that I have created a balance between expository texts and fiction.

Key Questions

• How can I insert consistent experiences with nonfiction into every literacy structure? Some of the formats and tools follow:

	POSSIBILITIES
Read aloud	Read expository picture books, *Ranger Rick Magazine*, *Time for Kids*, news articles, *Sports Illustrated for Kids*, science books, biographies, memoirs, math story problems, newspapers
Shared book	Nonfiction big books, charts, poems, descriptions, directions, transparencies, poems about real things, news articles, pages from textbooks, pages from nonfiction magazines
Small-group experiences, guided reading, literature circles, reciprocal teaching	Multiple copy sets of nonfiction books, magazines, newspapers
Independent reading	Anything real! Newspapers, travel brochures, movie reviews, magazines, nonfiction books, familiar expository big books

Please also refer to *Revisit, Reflect, Retell* (Hoyt, 1999), Chapter 4, for a wide range of instructional opportunities and assessment tools for expository texts.

FIGURE 8.1 Partners working with an informational text.

Using a Table of Contents

I start this minilesson by talking about purposes for reading and then do a think aloud on how my strategies change, depending on my purpose.

Expository Text for Relaxation

I show the students how, during a time when I am relaxing with a book, I might look through the table of contents just to give myself an idea of the contents, then I slowly page through the text. Sometimes I read all the pages. Sometimes I read a bit, turn a few pages just looking at pictures, and then read some more when I see something that interests me. Sometimes I change the order all around. I might see something in the table of contents that really catches my eye and it is in the middle of the book. I could start in the middle, then return to the contents and select another part of the book or magazine to explore.

Expository Text for Quick Searches

I also show the students how, when I am searching for an answer, I use the table of contents to quickly find the section I need, skim and scan, and then leave the book. I personally use this kind of reading when I am researching and need a quick answer so I can return to my writing or to a discussion. I might use this kind of reading with a manual such as a computer manual or the manual to my car. It would be very rare for me to pick up the manual to my computer and read it from cover to cover, but I do appreciate it when I need to find an answer quickly.

To personalize this lesson, I ask the students to follow the same process I just used. If this minilesson is part of independent reading, I might ask them to attempt to use my relaxed reading style when using the table of contents. If this minilesson is part of small-group reading instruction or shared book experience, I might ask them to use my quick search style of using the table of contents to look for an answer to a question.

To further solidify understanding, I ask the students to work in teams to take an informational text that does not have a table of contents and to create one. (I am sincerely surprised at how often I pick up an expository big book or set of guided reading books on a nonfiction topic and do not see a table of contents.) Once they have done this a few times, it becomes a really meaningful choice to add to our Kidshop list of reading options, and soon the room is full of books with student-authored tables of contents.

Extensions

Ask students to review student-authored books that have been completed as well as those in production. Are there any that would benefit from a table of contents?

Key Questions

- How does your purpose affect your use of the table of contents?
- How can a table of contents help you as a reader?

Word Sorts to Stimulate and Build Prior Knowledge

I introduce this minilesson by placing individual words on pieces of sentence strips into a large pocket chart. The words have all come from an expository reading selection. If the topic is pumpkins, the words you select might include:

| Pumpkin | Farm | Vine | Leaves | Seeds | Orange |

| Jack-o-Lantern | Halloween | Pie | Pulp | Pick | Farmer | Pumpkin Patch |

Sorting

I show the students how to rearrange the words into categories. For example, I might group *seeds* and *pulp* together because they are inside of the pumpkin. I might group *pumpkin, pumpkin patch, farmer, pick, Halloween*, and *farm* together because those are all things that go with visiting a pumpkin patch on Halloween, and so on. Words can be used more than once. The objective is to look for categories and relationships between words, then to explain why these words go together. This activates prior knowledge and naturally assists the students in making connections between their understandings and the text.

Making Predictions

Next, they make predictions about the text the words have come from. Is it expository or narrative? What might be the major themes? What questions do they hope to have answered?

When students move from the word sort to reading the selection, the key vocabulary is ready to use and the conceptual understandings that are critical to making meaning are activated.

Variations

- Place the words on the overhead projector.
- Provide teams with sets of words to categorize.
- Have a group of students preview a text and select key words to present to students who have not yet seen the text.

Extensions

After reading, have the students look at the words again. How might they arrange the words now? Could they use the words to support a retell of the content? If they had been selecting the words, were there any others that were really important to the content? Were all of the words used in the text?

Key Questions

- How do my experiences and my understandings affect my reading?
- What can I do before reading to help myself understand?
- If I preview a text, can I pull out a few key words and think about categories, relationships, and what I already know?
- What have I learned about helping myself understand nonfiction?

Word Sorts to Stimulate and Build Prior Knowledge

joints	deep roots	kills crops	fragrant flowers
vine	hairy arms	fast growing	provides shade
big leaves	dense	aerates	break up hard soil
from Japan	web	legume	food for animals

© 2000 by Linda Hoyt from *Snapshots*. Portsmouth, NH: Heinemann.

Word Sorts to Stimulate and Build
Prior Knowledge

Hairy Green Pest

In 1876 a plant was brought to the United States from Japan as a gift. It had trailing vines, fragrant purple and violet flowers, and large leaves. The plant was welcomed into the southern United States, as it could quickly climb up porches and provide shade in the summer.

The plant is called Kudzu and we now know that it is the fastest growing vine of all. It grows up to a foot a day and can easily wrap around trees, cars, houses, and anything that gets in its way. As it grows, Kudzu extends hairy arms that are covered with green leaves as big as a human hand. Each Kudzu arm has joints called nodes. The nodes grow more hairy arms and form a dense web that is so strong it can pull down telephone poles, kill fruit trees and forests, and quickly take over a farmer's field.

Kudzu isn't all bad, however. It is a legume and a cousin to the common pea plant many people grow in their gardens. It has roots that can go as far as seven feet down and break up hard soil and aerate the ground to make the soil better for farming. It is also good food for animals. Chickens, cows, goats, and pigs like to eat it raw. When it is cooked, it tastes like cabbage.

The Challenge
How can farmers take advantage of Kudzu's benefits and still control it?

Use the blank word sort chart to brainstorm.

 © 2000 by Linda Hoyt from *Snapshots*. Portsmouth, NH: Heinemann.

Word Sort Template

© 2000 by Linda Hoyt from *Snapshots*. Portsmouth, NH: Heinemann.

Expository Reading Strategies Bookmark

This minilesson starts with a class exploration of expository texts. I invite the students to gather lots of examples of expository texts and then have an "expository read in" to begin to sort out the varying strategies they employ with varying texts.

T-Charts

I give each student or teams of students a chart such as the following:

TEXT READ	STRATEGIES USED

As they read a travel brochure, for example, student think about their approach to the text. What did they do? Did it give them the information they needed? Then students make notes in the strategies used column.

Class Chart

Next, a class chart is started to reflect the texts reviewed and the variety of strategies employed by the group with each kind of text.

The last step is to have students reflect personally on the strategies on the class list and make a list of the strategies each person believes will be most helpful. They record these strategies on personal expository bookmarks (see next snapshot) and start reading. At the end of each reading session, they are asked to review their bookmark strategies to consider any additions or deletions that may be helpful.

Key Questions

- Which kinds of text am I most likely to read?
- What strategies are most helpful to me in those texts?
- Am I remembering to continue to add strategies to my list?

Expository Reading Strategies Bookmark

Expository Bookmark

- Look at the pictures

- Look at the title

- Look at captions and bold type

- Make a picture in your mind

- Predict: Make smart guesses

- Think of I Wonder questions

- Skim

- Go back and really read

- Summarize in your head

- Make sense!

- Chunk challenging words; list the tricky ones

- Connect to what you know

Expository Bookmark

Good Reader Strategies

_____

_____

_____

_____

_____

_____

_____

_____

_____

© 2000 by Linda Hoyt from *Snapshots*. Portsmouth, NH: Heinemann.

Getting the Most from Pictures

During this minilesson, I make an overhead transparency of the pictures and text from the following page and assist the students in talking about the visual aspects of the layout. It is important to notice that expository text is laid out differently than narrative. In this case, the pictures carry as much information as the text and are arranged in a format that encourages the reader to look at the two-page spread as one connected visual image. I also show them how the text is designed to help you understand the picture better and to encourage you to look more closely at the pictures.

As we look at the layout, I do a think aloud to show the students my observations about the pictures and begin a list of I Wonder questions that the page brings to mind.

I next send the students on a text hunt to gather expository samples where the pictures and the text are connected and to do think alouds for each other.

For the personal think alouds, I ask them to meet with a partner and share their book by identifying a page with an interesting layout and to do a think aloud about what they observe and to develop I Wonder questions.

Variation

Expository texts often have boldfaced headings. Have the students create headings for each section of the text.

Key Questions

- What do writers of expository texts do to bring our attention to the pictures?
- What can we learn about layout that could be transferred to our own writing?
- How do the pictures and visual images affect my understanding?
- What does a writer do to draw the reader back to the pictures?

The clownfish hides
in the tentacles
to keep safe.

FIGURE 8.2 Pages from *The Coral Reef*. Reprinted with permission from *The Coral Reef* by Christine Economos.

Getting the Most from Pictures

Orange and white clownfish live here.
They stay near an animal
with green tentacles.
Can you see the green tentacles?

FIGURE 8.3 A full-size version of *The Coral Reef*.

Reprinted with permission from *The Coral Reef* by Christine Economos, New York, Newbridge Publications.

Cloze with Nonfiction

Make a transparency of the following page and cover key words with sticky notes. Ask the students to consider words that might be hiding under the sticky notes. As they suggest words, it is important to continually ask: Why do you think so? After meaningful words are suggested, ask the students to predict the beginning sound, then slide the sticky note aside to uncover the first letter and ask if the children still think their word is going to fit. Does the beginning sound match their prediction? What other letters do they think they will see? and so on.

Key Questions

- Can you predict words in information books?
- Do good reader strategies work in information books the same way they work in stories?
- Are there any good reader strategies that are different in information books?

Lions

Who takes care of
these babies?

FIGURE 8.4 Page from *Taking Care of Baby*. Reprinted with permission from *Taking Care of Baby* by Daniel Jacobs, New York, Newbridge Publications (Discovery Links).

Cloze with Nonfiction

Two mothers team up.
They help each other take care
of their cubs.

FIGURE 8.5 Full-size version of *Taking Care of Baby.*

Reprinted with permission from *Taking Care of Baby* by Daniel Jacobs, New York, Newbridge Publications (Discovery Links).

© 2000 by Linda Hoyt from *Snapshots*. Portsmouth, NH: Heinemann.

Table of Contents Predictions

Reprinted with permission from *Amazing Sharks* by Melvin Berger, New York: Newbridge Publishing (1996).

Think Aloud: Before Reading

BEFORE READING Content Predictions	Word Predictions	AFTER READING Reflections
What do I think I will learn?	Name specific words you think will appear.	Key words and Ideas
Page 1 General ideas	shark, ocean	
Page 2 Names of sharks	hammerhead, nurse,	
Page 6 Size and shape	Mouth, body, fins	

AFTER READING: REFLECTIONS		
Check concepts and words which appeared in the book and add key ideas and words you learned.		

BEFORE READING Content Predictions	Word Predictions	AFTER READING Reflections
What do I think I will learn?	Name specific words you think will appear.	Key words and Ideas
Page 1 General ideas	√shark, √ocean	Great White
Page 2 √Names of sharks	√hammerhead, nurse body	Prehistoric
Page 6 √Size and shape	√Mouth, √body, √fins	Move to breathe

Table of Contents Predictions

	BEFORE READING Content Predictions	Word Predictions	AFTER READING Reflections
	What do I think I will learn?	Name specific words you think will appear.	Key words and ideas
Chapter			
Chapter			
Chapter			

Now . . . read a chapter to cross-check your predictions. After reading, put a check next to the words and ideas that actually appeared in the text and add key ideas and words you learned.

© 2000 by Linda Hoyt from *Snapshots*. Portsmouth, NH: Heinemann.

Go for the Gold!

In the Go for the Gold! strategy students learn to analyze text and attempt to summarize the significant ideas in just a few words. The idea is to target words that bring on larger images, hit generalizations and big ideas, and represent the most critical understandings. By limiting the number of words students can select, they must weed out lesser details and focus on the most important concepts.

Key Words

In this strategy, students list key words to the side of the passage, much like in the key word strategy from Chapter 7 on independent reading. Then, readers analyze the key words to determine which ONE is really the most important. They write this word on a gold-colored card or square of paper and then select three to five additional words that help to capture the essence of the passage.

My demonstration of the Go for the Gold! strategy models how I consider which words are most important and make my decisions. I think aloud about how I first choose key words, then come back and review the passage to select the gold word, and then the three to five supporting words. After selecting the Go for the Gold! words, I read the passage again to ensure that I am still happy with my choices.

Students enjoy sharing their Go for the Gold! cards with each other and delight in explaining the words they have chosen and why they selected them.

The transparency on the next page could support your think aloud or student practice of the strategy. I like to follow the demonstration with immediate practice in a textbook or other informational text. Following the gradual release of responsibility model, I then would plan for teams of two to four to work together and then move to individual practice.

Sample

	Go for the Gold!
Eagles	Eagle—Bird
Habitat	*Support Words*
Eagles build their nest in tall trees, cliff ledges,	nests, high, keep
or in other high, private places. They weave	
twigs and sticks together then line the nest	
with leaves, moss, grass, feathers, and pine	
needles. They often keep the nest for many	
years and continue to add to it. Fish and sea	
eagles have built nests that measure as much	
as twenty feet high and eight feet across.	

This strategy is also a strong foundation for a conversation on how to avoid plagiarism in your writing.

Key Questions

- How do I identify the most important ideas when I read?
- Can words and phrases really help me remember?
- How could I use the key word strategy when I am reading on my own?
- How might the key word strategy help when I am doing research for writing?

FIGURE 8.6 Students working on a Go for the Gold! lesson.

Go for the Gold! Strategy

Go for the Gold! Word
_____

Support Words
_____
_____
_____

Eagles

Habitat

Eagles build their nest in tall trees, cliff ledges, or in other high, private places. They weave twigs and sticks together then line the nest with leaves, moss, grass, feathers, and pine needles. They often keep the nest for many years and continue to add to it. Fish and sea eagles have built nests that measure as much as twenty feet high and eight feet across.

Dangers to Eagles

If left alone in the wild, eagles could live up to forty years. But too many come close to civilization and are dying because trees have been cut down and water poisoned with fertilizers and pesticides. Others are killed by electricity lines, traps meant for other animals, and accidental shootings. We currently have only half as many eagles in the world as there were 100 years ago.

© 2000 by Linda Hoyt from *Snapshots*. Portsmouth, NH: Heinemann.

Skim and Scan It Checklist

Reader _____   Text _____

Strategies Used

I utilized the table of contents	yes	no
I skimmed quickly to get the big idea	yes	no
I looked for key words	yes	no
I used illustrations/charts/graphs	yes	no
I made predictions	yes	no
I thought of a question and skimmed to find an answer	yes	no
I read the questions at the end of the chapter and then skimmed for answers	yes	no
I read the first sentence in each paragraph then skimmed the paragraph to get the gist	yes	no
After skimming a paragraph, I went back and read it slowly for details	yes	no
After skimming a paragraph, I thought of a "test" question someone might ask on this topic	yes	no
I used the index	yes	no

The benefits of skimming are:

_____

I think I should use it when:

_____

_____

© 2000 by Linda Hoyt from *Snapshots*. Portsmouth, NH: Heinemann.

Map It Out Strategy

The Main Idea: ⟶

Key Points:

- _____
- _____
- _____
- _____

My Summary:

_____

_____

_____

_____

_____

_____

_____

© 2000 by Linda Hoyt from *Snapshots*. Portsmouth, NH: Heinemann.

Dealing with Directions

Recipe for a Peanut Butter and Jelly Sandwich

First you _____ the jar of peanut butter.

Then you open the jar of _____.

Next you _____ spread peanut
b_____ on one slice of bread.

After that, you spread jelly on one _____
of bread.

Finally, you put the two slices together and take a
big _____! YUM!

© 2000 by Linda Hoyt from *Snapshots*. Portsmouth, NH: Heinemann.

Writing Your Own Directions

Try the same format to tell how to do something else!

First _____

_____

Then _____

_____

Next _____

_____

After that _____

_____

Finally _____

_____

© 2000 by Linda Hoyt from *Snapshots*. Portsmouth, NH: Heinemann.

Gotcha!

In this minilesson, I demonstrate how to develop questions based on a passage. I emphasize question quality and hitting the important issues, rather than unimportant details.

Team Format

The students meet in teams to read a passage, then write questions about it. At an agreed upon time, students trade papers and attempt to answer each other's questions.

Variations

For independent practice, students could develop questions about independent reading books and slide the questions into the books for future readers to enjoy.

Key Questions

- Which questions get to the important ideas?
- Are some questions better than others?
- How do my questions compare to the questions written by others?
- How do my questions compare to those written in textbooks?
- How do my questions compare to those on standardized tests?

FIGURE 8.7 Students working on a Gotcha! lesson.

Title It

Show the students a copy of a newspaper and begin reading the titles of articles. Do not read the articles themselves. Invite a conversation. What do you notice about the titles? Do they sound like titles for books? How are they different? What are the attributes of a newspaper title? What is the purpose for the title?

Writing Our Own Titles

Could we create interesting titles about events at school? Examples: Boy Chokes on Banana, Volunteers Read with Kindergartners, Principal Wows Students, Power Fails at Elementary School, etc. How about titles for events in your personal lives? Examples: Boy Flies to Montana, Wedding Runs Amok, Dog Races from Cat!

News Articles

Make a transparency of the following page then cut the articles and titles apart. Using a highlighter, show the students how you quickly skim an article, select a key word or idea, then identify the title. Or, start with the titles, predict key ideas, and decide if that is an article you would like to read.

Provide an opportunity for students to work with news articles. To set this up, I cut articles from the newspaper and remove the title from each article. Teams then work to skim the articles, highlighting a key word or two. Then, they identify the titles that would match each article. I keep an original, uncut copy of the newspaper available so they can check their work. It is helpful to explain to the students that this exercise is helping them to skim and scan, search for main ideas, select key words, and understand the genre.

Key Questions

- What is the function of titles in newspapers?
- How do the titles affect readers?
- What are the clues in titles that tell us about the content?
- What could we learn about writing good titles?
- Could we use what we know about titles to write better leads in our writing?

Title It

A SIMPLE SEAT
ADJUSTMENT
SOUNDS KINDA FUN

*Violent winds and massive
tidal surges hamper the setup
of a custom-made barrier net
for the orca in an Iceland bay*

LOOKING FOR
A NEEDLE
IN THE
BRAINSTEM

Well, the weather outside is frightful and the landscape somewhat less than delightful.

Those two harsh realities of winter in Iceland have delayed progress — but apparently not dimmed hopes — in the effort to reintroduce Keiko the famous killer whale to the wild.

Caretakers had planned late this fall to string a barrier net across the entrance to the bay in which the whale's holding pen is anchored and, by Christmas, to allow him out of the pen and into the enclosed bay — an intermediate step between captivity and release. But mighty winds, heavy snows and uncooperative geology have pushed keepers' estimate of Keiko's first bay swim to mid-January at the earliest.

When the day comes, the orca star of the popular 1993 movie "Free Willy" will swim through a steel gate in his pen and have about 800,000 square feet of bay in which to stretch his muscular flukes and explore.

The good news on pain is that acupuncture relieves it and a scan of brain activity proves it. Reporting to the Radiological Society of North America, doctors at the University of Medicine and Dentistry of New Jersey said: "So many people with pain, whether from cancer, headache or a chronic, unexplained condition, rely on medications, such as morphine, which can become addicting. Acupuncture has no side effects, and … the pain relief it provides can last for months."

When you're ready to ride that new bike that was under the tree, you might want to think about this: A simple seat adjustment could ease back pain caused by cycling. In a report in the British Journal of Sports Medicine, Israeli researchers say dipping the saddle forward 10 to 15 degrees reduces muscle strain and realigns the bones. Up to 70 percent of cyclists suffer from back pain that the researchers believe is caused, at least in part, when the angle between the pelvis and the lower end of the spinal column is overextended. The researchers say the findings could be particularly important for children, because tension between the spine and pelvis could interfere with growth. And, it goes without saying, wear your danged helmet. Yes, we mean you!

FIGURE 8.8 Text and titles used with permission of *The Oregonian*, 1999.

© 2000 by Linda Hoyt from *Snapshots*. Portsmouth, NH: Heinemann.

Pick a Word (Inferential Reasoning)

In this minilesson, I demonstrate what I call the Two Word Strategy (*Revisit, Reflect, Retell*, Hoyt, 1999, page 4) and explain to students that meaning actually comes from merging the words of the passage with the ideas in our head.

For example: Either read this article aloud or make a transparency of the text.

Girl Scouts Help Out City's Homeless

Local Girl Scouts in Portland have chosen to give up part of their Christmas Day celebrations with their families to serve breakfast and distribute warm clothes to homeless people in downtown Portland. More than 400 homeless people attended the breakfast. One parent said, "This helps our girls to see their world more realistically and builds a positive attitude about helping their community."

Two-Word Strategy

Think about the article. Jot down two words that reflect your thinking. Be ready to tell why you chose the words.

WORDS	WHY YOU CHOSE THEM
Need	I chose it because there are so many homeless people who need this
Important	I chose important because it is so important for everyone to help others.

Generally, students select words that are inferences, reflecting judgment, conclusions, and evaluations that move beyond the text.

In the Pick a Word Strategy, I ask them to choose only one word and write it on a 3 × 5 card. On the back of the card, they write WHY they chose the word. The cards are passed around the group and students talk together about the words they are reading and how they relate to the text.

The Pick a Word and Two-Word Strategies both scaffold inferential reasoning, which is almost always represented on standardized tests. These strategies are quick, adjustable to various groups sizes, and work with any text.

Key Questions

- How do you merge the words of the text and the ideas in your head?
- Are there other ways to represent inferential thinking?
- How might Two Word and Pick a Word help me understand when I am reading independently?

Pick a Word

1. Jot down two words that reflect your thinking about the passage.

   _____   _____

2. Tell why you chose them.

3. Pick ONE word and write it on a 3 × 5 card. On the back, tell why you chose it and how it relates to the story. Meet with your group to share your words and your reasons for selecting them.

© 2000 by Linda Hoyt from *Snapshots*. Portsmouth, NH: Heinemann.

The Third Time Around

This is a group strategy for dealing with expository selections for emergent to proficient readers. In this strategy, each student needs a personal copy of the text, sticky notes, and paper for writing questions.

First Time Around: Skim and Scan

What do you notice?

What do you think will be the key ideas?

What words do you predict?

Second Time Around: Read for Details

Read slowly.

Identify key words and ideas.

Use sticky notes to mark points.

Talk:

Reach agreement on the important points.

Third Time Around: Synthesize

Quiz yourself.

Write questions that could be on a test.

Think and talk: Why is this information important?

Think and Read Poster

Prereading Thoughts

Preview the passage.

What do you think it will be about?

What are some things you already know on the topic?

What do you hope to learn from this passage?

How will you use what you learn? (take a test, answer questions, do a retell)

What strategies could you use while you read to help yourself remember?

How will you know if you understood?

During Reading Thoughts

What are the main ideas so far?

What kind of graphic organizer might help you collect information?

What picture do you have in your mind?

Is the information similar to anything you have learned before?

What are you wondering?

What questions do you have?

Are you using good reader strategies on challenging words?

What strategies have you used so far?

After Reading Thoughts

Main ideas?

What else do you want to know?

How will you help yourself remember?

Which reading strategies did you use? Which were most helpful?

What parts interested you the most?

© 2000 by Linda Hoyt from *Snapshots*. Portsmouth, NH: Heinemann.

9

. . . .

Writing
Collecting My Thoughts, Telling
My Stories, Moving Forward
as a Writer

In writing, minilessons are the heartbeat of the workshop, the fine-tuning of the craft. But, minilessons in writing can also remind us of the many forms for writing and the tools we have to help ourselves as writers. Tools for self-reflection, tools for learning from our peers, and tools for learning from the craft of published authors all have a place in the realm of minilessons for writing.

As in all other dimensions of my literacy instruction, I provide supports to writers by first getting to know them as people and then evaluating their strengths as writers. Writing tells me about children's interests, their knowledge of phonics, of syntax and grammar, of conventions, and so much more.

As I review a child's writing, the observation tool on the following page can be helpful.

Writing Self-Evaluation Chart

Name _____

I can . . .

	DATE	DATE	DATE
Draw a picture	❏	❏	❏
Write beginning sounds	❏	❏	❏
Write my name	❏	❏	❏
Write ending sounds	❏	❏	❏
Write some sounds in the middle of words	❏	❏	❏
Leave spaces between words	❏	❏	❏
Write words other people can read	❏	❏	❏
Write about my pictures	❏	❏	❏
Use periods	❏	❏	❏
Use question marks	❏	❏	❏
Capitalize first letters in sentences	❏	❏	❏
Capitalize names of people and places	❏	❏	❏
Read my writing to see if it makes sense	❏	❏	❏
Give a lot of information	❏	❏	❏
Write a story with a beginning, middle, and end	❏	❏	❏
Write descriptions	❏	❏	❏
Write notes	❏	❏	❏
Write facts	❏	❏	❏
Write letters	❏	❏	❏

Continues

© 2000 by Linda Hoyt from *Snapshots*. Portsmouth, NH: Heinemann.

Writing Self-Evaluation Chart *continued*

	DATE	DATE	DATE
Write to persuade	❏	❏	❏
Write to inform	❏	❏	❏
Cut and paste to add information	❏	❏	❏
Make changes after I read to a friend	❏	❏	❏
Look for words I think are not spelled correctly	❏	❏	❏
Fix my spelling with help from a friend	❏	❏	❏
Use the word wall to help me spell	❏	❏	❏
Write titles for my writing	❏	❏	❏
Try not to start sentences with AND	❏	❏	❏
Use question marks	❏	❏	❏
Indent for paragraphs	❏	❏	❏
Write interesting leads	❏	❏	❏
Think of endings that make sense with my story	❏	❏	❏
Use interesting words	❏	❏	❏
Think about my audience	❏	❏	❏
Make sure my writing is FINE	❏	❏	❏
Factual	❏	❏	❏
Interesting	❏	❏	❏
Neat	❏	❏	❏
Effort is shown!	❏	❏	❏
This student is interested in:	❏	❏	❏

© 2000 by Linda Hoyt from *Snapshots*. Portsmouth, NH: Heinemann.

Note Writing and List Making

This minilesson is focused on the many reasons people write both in and away from school. I start by telling the students that I am going to think really hard about the things I have written in the last day or two and then I begin making a list of my reasons to write. My list might include:

- grocery list
- to do list
- list of things to take to the beach
- list of bills I need to pay
- list of phone calls I need to make
- a friend's telephone number
- addressing an envelope
- lesson plans
- note to my husband
- note to my daughter
- note to the principal
- note to a student
- letter to parents, and so on

As I continue to reflect, I could mention to the students that it appears that lists and notes happen a lot in my daily life as a writer. I then go on to demonstrate list making or note writing using the following transparency, and ask the students how we might use lists and notes in the classroom.

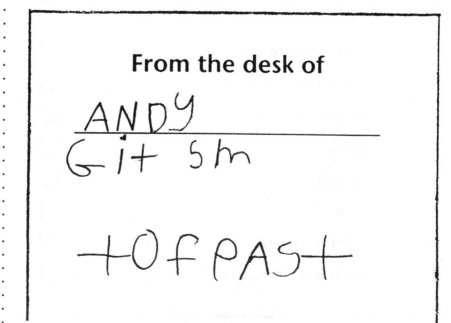

From the desk of

ANDY
Git sm

tOfPAst

FIGURE 9.1 Sample of note pads and lists.

After demonstrating note writing and list making on the overhead projector, I encourage the students to try to integrate note writing and list making into our classroom. When someone comes to tell me we have run out of paper towels, for example, I could then respond: "Could you take a minute to write me a note. That will really help me remember." If a student says, "Don't forget that today is the bus drill." I can respond, "Would you make a list of the things we need to do this morning and make sure the bus drill appears on the list so we don't forget."

Key Questions

- How can lists help me organize my time?
- How might lists help me remember things I need to do?
- How could notes help me communicate better with my parents, my teacher, my friends?

Note Writing and List Making

From the desk of _____

( ) note   ( ) list

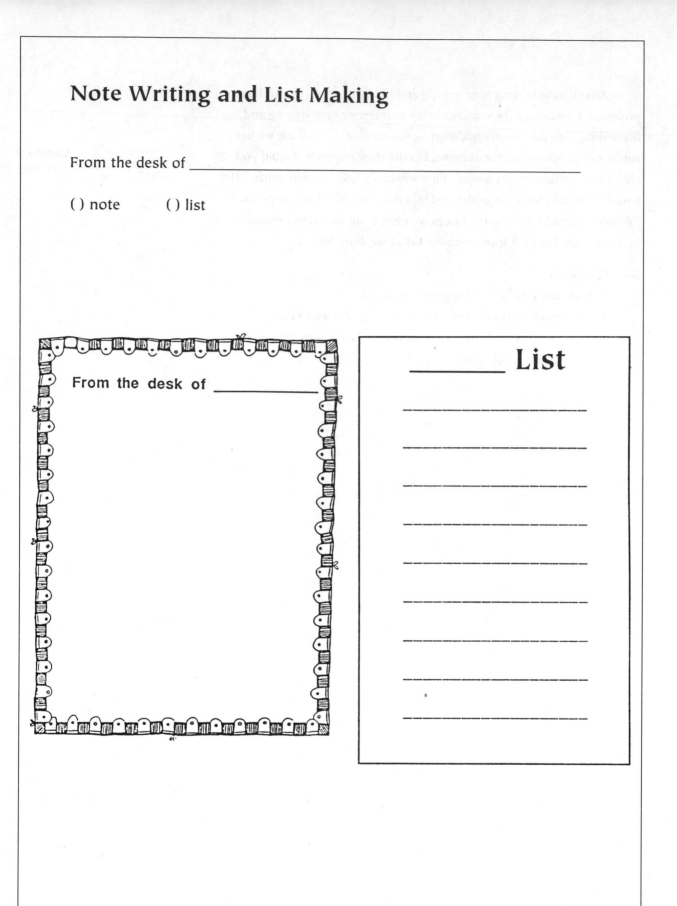

From the desk of _____

_____ List

_____
_____
_____
_____
_____
_____
_____
_____
_____

© 2000 by Linda Hoyt from *Snapshots*. Portsmouth, NH: Heinemann.

Parents as Partners in Reflection

Once a month, I have children select a "best piece of work" to celebrate. The chosen piece of writing does not have to be published, just something the student has reason to take pride in.

Making a Selection

To initiate this process, I take my own writing folder and think aloud about the pieces inside. I tell the students how I feel about some of the pieces, for instance why some are special sources of pride. Then I select one piece to really spend time reflecting on.

I read the piece aloud, think about it for a bit, and then begin writing a self-reflection on the transparency that follows this page. I start the reflection: "I am proud of this because _____ ." While writing, I think aloud about the importance of being specific. It isn't helpful to say I am proud of this because it is good. It is helpful to say I am proud of it because of my word choices, for example. I might say "I really feel good about using the word *tumbled* instead of *fell* and about using *growled* instead of *said*."

Involving Families

After modeling for the students, I explain that we are going to begin sharing our reflections with our families so they will need to follow the same process I used. They need to:

1. Look through your writing folder.
2. Select a piece you are particularly proud of.
3. Reflect on what you did in the piece, be specific.
4. Write your reflection. Remember that the teacher and your parents will be adding their observations.

This process can form the backbone of a traveling folder that goes home each month and gives the parents a sense of involvement in supporting their child as well as a window into their child's development as a writer.

Key Questions

- What can I learn from my reflections on my writing?
- How could I use the feedback I get from my teacher and my parents to improve my writing?

Parents as Partners in Reflection

Date:_____ Author:_____ Title of Writing:_____

I am proud of this because . . .
(The Student) _____
                        name

_____

_____

_____

I am proud of this because . . .
(The Teacher)_____
                        name

_____

_____

_____

I am proud of this because . . .
(The Parent) _____
                        name

_____

_____

_____

_____

© 2000 by Linda Hoyt from *Snapshots*. Portsmouth, NH: Heinemann.

The Punctuation Song

To assist children in remembering rules for punctuation, I teach them this song to the tune of "Clementine (Oh, my darling . . .)" and then actually hum it while I edit a piece of writing on the overhead. It is fun and useful!

PUNCTUATION

Names and places, beginning of sentences

All deserve a capital

Periods come at ends of sentences or

abbreviations

Commas are a little harder

They can leave us feeling blue

They are used in a greeting, in a list, or with

a phrase.

Punctuation, Punctuation

We are trying hard to learn

These rules can make us crazy

But with patience we can learn

© 2000 by Linda Hoyt from *Snapshots*. Portsmouth, NH: Heinemann.

Revising with Scissors

Some writers are hesitant to revise because they get frustrated squeezing information into small spaces or having to spend time recopying their work to create room to add details and expand thoughts.

I like to teach a strategy I learned from a wonderful principal and colleague, Robin Case. She taught me to revise with scissors!

Getting Started

I start by placing a piece of writing on the overhead projector and reading it aloud. I then think aloud about the piece. Do I have questions for the author? Is there any place in the piece where I wish I could hear more? Are there any ideas that should be together but actually appear in different parts of the story?

Using the transparency of writing on the next page, you could follow this process with an array of questions: Where is Diamond Lake? The house sounds interesting. What else do we wonder about the house? The part about the dock is amazing. I wonder how his Uncle caught the fish with his hand?

Scissor Time

I can now take scissors and cut the sentences apart. Are there any sentences that seem to go together? I could reflect that "Yes, the dock and the catching of the fish go together but we want to know so much more!" If you use clear tape and tape those two sentences to the top of a new transparency or paper, there is lots of room to add the new ideas.

Are there any sentences that don't seem like they fit this story and might be saved for another piece? I could reflect that "Yes, the part about the house and the boat don't seem to fit," so those sentences could be taped to the top of a new page and expanded another time.

By cutting and taping sentences onto new paper with room to expand key ideas, writers are free to revise without stress.

For guided and independent practice, I ask writers to select a piece of writing in their folder and try Revising with Scissors to expand their ideas and give them a choice of working independently or with a partner.

Key Questions:

- How might I use Revising with Scissors to improve my own writing?
- Does this kind of revision work for me as a writer?
- How could I use this kind of revision to work on paragraphing?

Revising with Scissors

Diamond Lake by Kyle

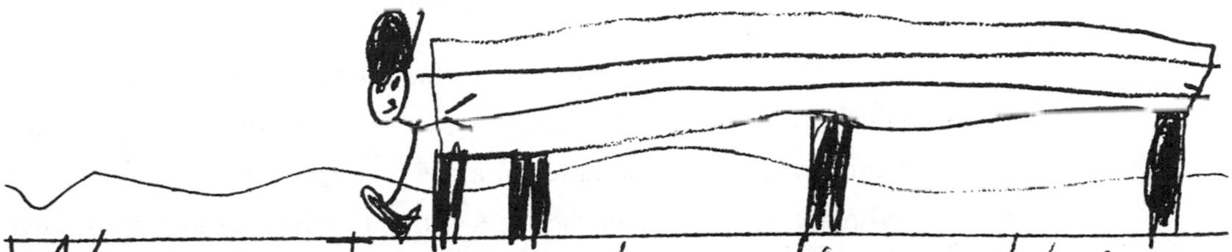

Wunts I went to dimund lake.
I stade in a house. I took my
boat. My uncle came with
me. Wen he was siting on the
tock. He saw a fish and then
he reched dawn and caught
fish With his hand.

Kyle

FIGURE 9.2 Kyle's Diamond Lake story.

© 2000 by Linda Hoyt from *Snapshots*. Portsmouth, NH: Heinemann.

Creating Interest with Words

This minilesson integrates easily into a big book cloze activity. I place a stack of at least ten sheets of sticky notes over a verb in a big book.

Example

"I am hungry," _____ the giant.

[stack of sticky notes]

I think out loud about words that might be used to finish the sentence, and write *said* on the top sticky note. The students and I then read it and consider if it makes sense. I peel that sticky note off of the stack and place it at the top of the page, asking the students to come up with another word that would work. We continue this process until meaningful words have been written on all ten sticky notes.

Now, we have an array of words that might include:

growled   grumbled   whispered   yelled   said   and so on

The next step is to rank the words in order of intensity. Which word is the most intense, least intense, and so on. Once the words are ranked, the students decide whether this passage calls for a word that is loud and intense or quiet, and make a final selection of the BEST word.

Guided Practice

Guided practice then involves giving students stacks of sticky notes and sending them to review a piece of writing, having them select one word to cover and then applying the process to come up with the best word ever!

Key Questions

- Which words express my meaning the best?
- Which words provide the best images for my reader?
- How can I select words that inform the reader and help to create an image?

Varying My Sentences

Using a piece of my own writing, I use the transparency on the following page to record the first word in each of my sentences and tell the students what I notice about my sentence beginnings. Do they start in the same ways? Is there a pattern to them?

I then might ask: "How else could I start two or three of these sentences so they don't sound so much the same?"

Thinking About Variation

After rewriting the beginning of one or two sentences, I then think aloud about sentence length.

> Are my sentences all the same length?
> Do they vary? Are some short and some long?
> How many times did I use the word AND?
> What do I observe about my sentences and what can I learn from my observations?

For independent practice, each student is given a sheet such as the one on the following page and an opportunity to reflect on his or her sentences.

Extra Reinforcement

If this is a confusing idea to students and they need multiple minilessons on the topic, I often read a favorite picture book and focus on the beginning of each sentence. What did this author do to make the sentence beginnings sound interesting? Can we try that in our writing? What do we notice about the author's sentence length?

Key Questions

- How can I make my sentences have variety and sound interesting?
- What do published authors to do make their sentence beginnings interesting?
- It is important to notice sentence length. How can I help myself remember?
- Are my sentences descriptive and communicate emotions?

Varying My Sentences

Name _____ Date _____ Title of Writing _____

Number of sentences _____

First word in each sentence

The number of times I used the word "and" _____

Number of sentences that are:

Long _____ Medium _____ Short _____

The sentence I like best_____

_____.

I like it because _____

_____.

My goal for improving my sentences would be _____

_____

_____

_____.

© 2000 by Linda Hoyt from *Snapshots*. Portsmouth, NH: Heinemann.

Peer Editing

To show that peer editing is helpful to all writers, I ask a student to be my peer reviewer and help me work with a piece of my writing in front of the class. I like to make a particular effort to turn to a student who isn't normally seen as a leader in writing so that the children can begin to understand that we can all make contributions in our efforts to support each other.

The Demonstration

It is helpful to have your writing sample written on chart paper or a transparency so that everyone can see and hear as you talk with your peer reviewer. I try to demonstrate that my partner and I will read the piece together and make some decisions about what to work on together and what I will do on my own. We can show our decisions on the form. During this time, I also try to demonstrate offering suggestions in a positive and constructive way and give the group an opportunity to practice offering suggestions to my work.

The checklist on the following page can support the demonstration as well as independent practice.

Key Questions

- Revision and editing can be done alone but you learn more with a partner.
- How can I make the best use of my partner's time?
- What should I do to be ready for a peer revising and editing conversation?
- How can I word suggestions so they are specific and helpful?
- How can I be sure that I am kind to the writer when I make suggestions?

Peer Editing Checklist

Author's name_____ Date _____

Partner's name_____ Title of writing _____

1. I read my rough draft to my partner _____ (date)

2. I am trying to revise for:
   ❑ creating visual images
   ❑ putting my ideas in a logical order
   ❑ adding interesting words
   ❑ varying sentence length
   ❑ varying sentence openings
   ❑ creating an interesting opening
   ❑ a strong ending
   ❑ telling enough information
   ❑ narrowing my topic
   My partner will help me with _____

   _____

3. Editing checklist
   ❑ Title is interesting and matches story
   ❑ Spelling edit completed   ❑ by myself   ❑ with my partner
   ❑ Periods, question marks and exclamation marks at ends of
      sentences
   ❑ Capital letters: beginning of sentence, names, dates
   ❑ Quotation marks around dialogue
   ❑ Other _____

4. Conference with my teacher. Date _____

5. Next steps: _____

   _____

© 2000 by Linda Hoyt from *Snapshots*. Portsmouth, NH: Heinemann.

Personal Writing Record

Name _____

Title of Writing	Genre	Date Started	Stages of the Process I Applied to This Piece				
			Draft	Revise Words	Revise Ideas	Edit	Publish

© 2000 by Linda Hoyt from *Snapshots*. Portsmouth, NH: Heinemann.

Antonym Antics

Sometimes it is helpful to demonstrate extremes in meaning to help students reflect on the messages they are creating in their writing. To create this demonstration for students, I read a passage that has some adjectives in it and then change every adjective to either an antonym or a word with a distinctly different meaning.

Example

The eensy weensy spider went up the water spout

Down came the rain and washed the spider out

Out came the sun and dried up all the rain

So, the eensy weensy spider went up the spout again.

IMAGES

What do you visualize?

Think Aloud

How could we change the image? What if the spider was going down the water spout? What image do you have in your head? What would help you get a sharper image?

Example

One day Andrew's mother bought him a nice, new blue sweater. When Andrew saw the sweater, he wanted to be nice, but somehow he just yelled, "That is ugly! If you think I am going to wear that you are crazy!"

IMAGES

What do you visualize?

Antonym Antics

LIST THE ADJECTIVES	LIST ANTONYMS
nice	mean
new	old
blue	
ugly	

If we change the image and use the antonyms, what might it sound like?

Key Questions

- How can we choose words that really clarify meaning?
- Is it ever helpful to use words that are extremes of meaning?
- Are there certain kinds of writing that use extremes?
- If I insert some antonyms into my writing, could I check to see if my original meaning was as clear as I thought it was?

Antonym Antics

IMAGES

Casual but classy

Easygoing but elegant. Most of all, our Missy Chenille
Sweater is so, so soft! It's the perfect
choice for the office or a holiday get-
together. It's thickness will keep you warm
during the chilly days ahead.

What do you visualize?

Think Aloud

How could you fine-tune the image? How could you change it to be oppo-site?

City view

Cozy and charming home in top location near downtown
with two bedrooms, one bathroom, a bonus room, close to
the river and a view of the mountain.

Think Aloud

How could you fine-tune the image? How could you change it to be oppo-site?

Uncomfortable and disgusting home in poor location far
from downtown. Far from the river and a view of the valley.

Use the newspaper and find other examples to use in Antonym Antics!

© 2000 by Linda Hoyt from *Snapshots*. Portsmouth, NH: Heinemann.

Dealing with Tired Words

Poetic language can help students push deeply into their vocabulary reserves and consider fresher word choices in their writing.

Said
To whisper
To say
To express
To shout
To grumble
To explain

Encourage your students to try this as a strategy for jazzing up their word choice and avoiding tired words.

Tired Word: _____

To _____

To _____

To _____

To _____

Key Questions
- Some words are overused. How can I help myself make better choices?
- When I feel challenged to think of fresher words, what can I do?

© 2000 by Linda Hoyt from *Snapshots*. Portsmouth, NH: Heinemann.

Managing Writers Workshop with a Planning Board

This planning board helps students remember the stages of the process by having them move a tongue depressor into library pockets to show the stage being addressed on a given day.

It also helps the teacher to create flexible groups that share a need to edit, choose a topic, revise, or tackle whatever task is required.

FIGURE 9.3 Writing with a planning board. The pockets read Prewrite, Draft, Revise, Edit, Publish, and Need Help.

Bibliography

Adams, Marilyn J. 1990. *Beginning to Read: Thinking and Learning About Print.* Cambridge, MA: MIT Press.

Allington, Richard. 1997. In *Building a Knowledge Base in Reading*, eds. Jane Braunger and Jan Lewis. Newark, DE: International Reading Association.

———. 1999. Presentation for staff in the Beaverton School District, Beaverton, Oregon. June 20, 1999.

Anderson, Richard, Paul Wilson, and Linda Fielding. 1988. "Growth in Reading and How Children Spend Their Time Outside of School." *Reading Research Quarterly* (Summer): 285–303.

Atwell, Nancie. 1998. *In the Middle: New Understandings About Writing, Reading, and Learning.* Portsmouth, NH: Heinemann

Billmeyer, R. and M. L. Barton. 1998. *Teaching Reading in the Content Area: If Not Me, Then Who?* Aurora, CO: Mid-Continent Regional Educational Laboratory.

Braunger, Jane, and Jan Lewis. 1997. *Building a Knowledge Base in Reading.* Newark, DE: International Reading Association.

Calkins, Lucy. 1986. *The Art of Teaching Writing.* Portsmouth, NH: Heinemann.

Calkins, Lucy, K. Montgomery, and D. Santman. 1998. *A Teacher's Guide to Standardized Testing: Knowledge Is Power.* Portsmouth, NH: Heinemann.

Cambourne, Brian. 1994. Presentation in the Beaverton School District, Beaverton, Oregon.

Caswell, Linda, and Nell K. Duke. 1998. "Non Narrative as a Catalyst for Literacy Development." *Language Arts* (February): 108–117.

Ciborowski, Jean. 1992. *Textbooks and the Students Who Can't Read Them.* Boston, MA: Brookline Books.

Clay, Marie. 1993. *An Observation Survey of Early Literacy Achievement.* Portsmouth, NH: Heinemann.

———. 1998. *Different Paths to Common Outcomes.* York, ME: Stenhouse.

Clymer, Theodore. 1963. "The Utility of Phonics Generalization in the Primary Grades." *The Reading Teacher* 16: 252–258.

Cooper, J. David. 1993. *Literacy: Helping Children Construct Meaning.* Boston, MA: Houghton Mifflin.

Culham, Ruth. 1998. *Picture Books: An Annotated Bibliography.* Portland, OR: Northwest Regional Educational Laboratory.

Cunningham, Patricia and Richard Allington. 1999. *Classrooms That Work: They Can All Read and Write.* New York: Longman.

Daniels, Harvey. 1994. *Literature Circles: Voice and Choice in the Classroom.* York, ME: Stenhouse.

Dionisio, Marie. 1998. "Teaching Reading Strategies in a Remedial Reading Class," ed. Weaver, Constance. *Practicing What We Know: Informed Reading Instruction.* Urbana, IL: National Council of Teachers of English.

Dowhower, Sarah L. 1999. "Supporting a Strategic Stance in the Classroom: A Comprehension Framework for Helping Teachers Help Students to Be Strategic." *The Reading Teacher* 52: 672–688.

Duke, Nell, 1999. "The Scarcity of Informational Reading in First Grade," CIERA Report, Center for the Improvement of Early Reading Instruction.

Education Department of Western Australia. 1995. *First Steps Reading Resource Book.* Portsmouth, NH: Heinemann.

Fiderer, Adele. 1997. *Mini-Lessons in Teaching Writing: Quick Lessons That Help Students Become Effective Writers.* New York: Scholastic.

Fletcher, Ralph. and Jean Portalupi. 1998. *Craft Lessons: Teaching Writing K–8.* York, ME: Stenhouse.

Fountas, Irene and Gay Su Pinnell. 1996. *Guided Reading: Good First Teaching for All Children.* Portsmouth, NH: Heinemann.

Goodman, Yetta, Dorothy Watson, and Carolyn Burke, 1996. *Reading Strategies: Focus on Comprehension, 2nd ed.* Katonah, NY: Richard C. Owen.

Graves, Michael and Bonnie Graves. 1994. *Scaffolding Reading Experiences.* Norwood, MA: Christopher Gordon.

Hall, Susan. 1994. *Using Picture Storybooks to Teach Literary Devices.* Phoenix, AZ: Oryx.

Harvey, Stephanie. 1998. *Nonfiction Matters: Reading, Writing and Research in Grades 3–8.* York, ME: Stenhouse.

Hoyt, Linda. 1995. *Accelerating Reading and Writing Success for At-Risk Learners.* Bellevue, WA: Bureau of Education and Research.

———. 1998. Video. Comprehension Strategies That Help Your Struggling Students Be More Successful Readers. Bellevue, WA: Bureau of Education and Research.

———. 1999. *Revisit, Reflect, Retell: Comprehension Strategies.* Portsmouth, NH: Heinemann.

International Reading Association and the National Association for the Education of Young Children (NAEYC). 1998. *Learning to Read and Write: Developmentally Appropriate Practices for Young Children.* Newark, DE: IRA.

Johnson, Janet. 1998. *Content Area Reading.* New York: Delmar.

Keene, Ellin and Susan Zimmerman. 1997. *Mosaic of Thought.* Portsmouth, NH: Heinemann.

Krashen, Stephen. 1993. *The Power of Reading: Insights from the Research.* Englewood, CO: Libraries Unlimited.

———. 1998. "Bridging Inequity with Books." *Educational Leadership* (January): 18–21.

Lane, Barry. 1993. *After the End: Teaching and Learning Creative Revision.* Portsmouth, NH: Heinemann.

McQuillan, Jeff. 1998. *The Literacy Crisis: False Claims, Real Solutions.* Portsmouth, NH: Heinemann.

Moline, Steve. 1995. *I See What You Mean: Children at Work with Visual Information.* York, ME: Stenhouse.

Moustafa, Margaret. 1997. *Beyond Traditional Phonics: Research Discoveries and Reading Instruction.* Portsmouth, NH: Heinemann.

National Center for Educational Statistics. 1999. "Executive Summary: NAEP 1998 Reading Report Card for the Nation and the States." Washington, DC: National Center for Education Statistics, U.S. Department of Education.

National Research Council. 1998. *Preventing Reading Difficulties in Young Children.* Washington, DC: National Academy Press.

Nagy, W., R. C. Anderson and P. Herman. 1987. "Learning Word Meanings from Context During Normal Reading." *American Educational Research Journal* 24: 237–270.

Nia, Isoke Titilayo. 1999. "Units of Study in the Writing Workshop." *Primary Voices*, 8 (1) (August).

Opitz, M. 2000. *Rhyme and Reason.* Portsmouth, NH: Heinemann.

Opitz, M. and T. Rasinski. 1999. *Good-Bye Round Robin.* Portsmouth, NH: Heinemann.

Pearson, P. D. 1999. Presentation for the Oregon Department of Education.

Pearson, P. D. and B. Taylor. 1999. *Schools That Beat the Odds.*

Pearson, P. D. and L. Fielding. 1991. "Comprehension Instruction." ed. R. Barr, M. Kamil, P. Mosenthan, and P. D. Pearson. *Handbook of Reading Research,* Vol. 2, pp 815–860. New York: Longman.

Pearson, P. D., L. Roehler, J. Dole, and G. Duffy. 1992. "Developing Expertise in Reading Comprehension," ed. J. Samuels and A. Farstrup. *What Research Has to Say About Reading Instruction.* Newark, DE: International Reading Association.

Pinnell, Gay Su and Fountas, Irene. 1998. *Word Matters: Teaching Phonics and Spelling in the Reading/Writing Classroom.* Portsmouth, NH: Heinemann.

Reduce, Ann Danon. 1999. "Genre Study of Nonfiction Writing: Feature Articles, Editorials, and Essays." *Primary Voices* (8) 1 (August).

Routman, Regie. 2000. *Conversations: Strategies for Teaching, Learning, and Evaluating.* Portsmouth, NH: Heinemann.

Schlick Noe, Katherine, and Nancy J. Johnson. 1999. *Getting Started with Literature Circles.* Norwood, MA: Christopher Gordon.

Short, Kathy, and Jerome Harste. 1996. *Creating Classrooms for Authors and Inquirers.* Portsmouth, NH: Heinemann.

Siera, M., and S. Siera. 1999. "Fact or Fiction: Elementary Teachers Use of Literature in the Classroom," in the *Northwest Reader.* Newport, OR: Oregon Reading Association.

Silverstein, Shel. 1974. *Where the Sidewalk Ends.* New York, NY: Harper and Rowe.

Snow, Catherine, M. Susan Burns, and Peg Griffin, eds. 1998. *Preventing Reading Difficulties in Young Children.* Washington, DC: National Academy Press.

Snowball, Diane. 1995. "Building Literacy Skills Through Nonfiction: Some Tips on How You Can Help Children Become Better Readers and Writers of Nonfiction." *Teaching K–8* (May): 62–63.

Stanovich, K. 1994. "Romance and Reality." *The Reading Teacher* 47: 280–291.

Traill, L. 1999. Presentation at the International Reading Association Conference, San Diego, California.

Viscovatti, Karen. 1998. "Developing Primary Voices," ed. Weaver, Connie. *Practicing What We Know: Informed Reading Instruction.* Urbana, IL: National Council of Teachers of English.

Vogt, Mary Ellen. 1998. Presentation for the Title I staff, Beaverton, Oregon School District.

Vygotsky, L. 1978. *Mind in Society.* Cambridge, MA: Harvard University Press.

Watson, Dorothy. 1978. "Reader Selected Miscues: Getting More from Sustained Silent Reading." *English Education* 10:75–85.

Weaver, Constance. 1998. *Practicing What We Know: Informed Reading Instruction.* Urbana, IL: National Council of Teachers of English.

———. 1998. *Reconsidering a Balanced Approach to Reading.* Urbana IL: National Council of Teachers of English.

Weaver, Constance, L. Gillmeister-Krause and G. Vento-Zogby. 1996. *Creating Support for Effective Literacy Education.* Portsmouth, NH: Heinemann.